A Play

by

JOHN OSBORNE

LUTHER

THE DRAMATIC PUBLISHING COMPANY

CAST

KNIGHT

PRIOR

MARTIN

HANS

LUCAS

WEINAND

TETZEL

STAUPITZ

CAJETAN

MILTITZ

LEO

ECK

KATHERINE

HANS, THE YOUNGER

AUGUSTINIANS, DOMINICANS,

HERALD, HUNTSMEN,

PEASANTS, NOBLEMEN, EMPEROR, ETC.

3

The world premiere of LUTHER took place at the Paris Festival of 1961 under the direction of Tony Richardson, with decor by Jocelyn Herbert, and starring Albert Finney. It opened at the Royal Court in London, then played at the Edinburgh Festival and returned to London's Phoenix Theatre.

On September 25, 1963, LUTHER opened at the St. James Theatre in New York, produced by the David Merrick Foundation, directed by Tony Richardson, with the original sets and costumes, and Albert Finney, John Moffatt and Peter Bull from the original cast. The production subsequently moved to the Lunt-Fontanne Theatre and in April commenced a twelve-week tour. The following season brought an extensive coast-to-coast tour with the original sets and staging, and Alan Bergmann as Luther.

This edition is based on the New York production, taking into account slight changes and adjustments made to accommodate various theatres and touring situations. Two falcons and three Russian wolfhounds were replaced by a hawk and two Irish wolfhounds. Two children in the original company appeared in the Tetzel retinue and later as pages in the Diet of Worms. The opening line of ten monks and the allocation of business in the first act is based on the touring production, as is the Diet of Worms entrance. Both sequences and the "Eine Feste Burg" can be enlarged according to the available cast. In New York, a broad flight of stairs into the orchestra pit was used for the entrance of the principals in the opening of Act III.

When casting is limited, principals from Acts II and III can double as monks in Act I with attention to wig and makeup change and the assignment of the least conspicuous business. Principal roles in such combination as Lucas and Eck or the Prior and Cajetan can and have been double cast. Caution should be used in combining certain rhetorical roles such as Tetzel and Leo.

Mitchell Erickson,
Production Stage Manager

ACT ONE

SCENE ONE: *The Convent of the Augustinian Order of Eremites at Erfurt. 1506.*

SCENE TWO: *The same. A year later.*

SCENE THREE: *Two hours later.*

ACT TWO

SCENE ONE: *The Market Place. Jütebog. 1517.*

SCENE TWO: *The garden of the Eremite Cloister. Wittenberg. 1517.*

SCENE THREE: *The Castle Church. Wittenberg. Eve of All Saints. 1517.*

SCENE FOUR: *The Fugger Palace. Augsburg. October 1518.*

SCENE FIVE: *A hunting lodge, Magliana, Italy. 1519.*

SCENE SIX: *Wittenberg. 1520.*

ACT THREE

SCENE ONE: *The Diet of Worms. 1521.*

SCENE TWO: *Wittenberg. 1525.*

SCENE THREE: *The Eremite Cloister, Wittenberg. 1530.*

NOTE: At the opening of most scenes, the Knight appears with helmet, gloves and banner, announces the time and place, then retires.

CHART OF STAGE POSITIONS

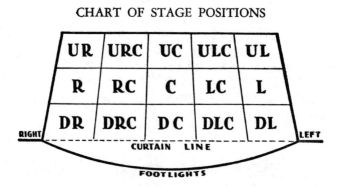

STAGE POSITIONS

Upstage means away from the footlights, *downstage* means toward the footlights, and *right* and *left* are used with reference to the actor as he faces the audience. R means *right*, L means *left*, U means *up*, D means *down*, C means *center*, and these abbreviations are used in combination, as: U R for *up right*, R C for *right center*, D L C for *down left center*, etc. One will note that a position designated on the stage refers to a general territory, rather than to a given point.

NOTE: Before starting rehearsals, chalk off your stage or rehearsal space as indicated above in the *Chart of Stage Positions*. Then teach your actors the meanings and positions of these fundamental terms of stage movement by having them walk from one position to another until they are familiar with them. The use of these abbreviated terms in directing the play saves time, speeds up rehearsals, and reduces the amount of explanation the director has to give to his actors.

ACT ONE

Scene One

SCENE: *The curtain rises on a darkened stage but for a shaft of light* D L. *In it stands the* KNIGHT, *helmeted, wearing gauntlets, and with a tall staff with trailing pennant.*]

KNIGHT. The Cloister Chapel of the Eremites of St. Augustine, Erfurt, Thuringia, the year of our Lord, fifteen hundred and six.

[*The* KNIGHT *exits* D L *and his light fades. The* Veni Creator *is heard offstage as the lights gradually build to a soft glow revealing an open set of towering walls which faintly suggest cloister arches and columns.* U C *hangs a gigantic crucifix. The body is emaciated, twisted and tortured, after a painting of the period by Mathias Grunewald.* U L *appears a line of monks in black cassock, scapular, cowl, and leather belt from which hangs a rosary. They sing from prayer books which are attached to the belt by a small chain. They wear sandals and have tonsure haircuts. Following the* PRIOR, *the monks and choir are as follows:*

MONK NO. 1: *Counter-tenor swinging censer with burning incense.*

MONK NO. 2: *Tenor carrying brass holy water bowl with twig.*

MONK NO. 3: (*Possible double casting for Act Two principal.*)

MONK NO. 4: *Carries Bible with marker for Martin's pledge.*

MONK NO. 5: *Acts as left dresser during investiture.*

MONK NO. 6: *Acts as right dresser during investiture.*

MONK NO. 7: *Brother Weinand carrying Martin's cassock, scapular, cowl, and belt.*

MONK NO. 8: *Bass.*

MONK NO. 9: *Baritone.*

7

MONK NO. 10: *Cantor (tenor)*.

The PRIOR *leads the line across the back, circling* D R *and then across the front. When he reaches* C, *the* PRIOR *breaks from the line and goes directly upstage to a position beneath the crucifix. He genuflects and faces front. The five monks immediately following the* PRIOR *continue across to left stage and then circle up to join the* PRIOR *at the center, forming the left arc of the semicircle. The last five monks hold in place stage right forming the right arc of the semicircle. The resultant formation is a large semicircle across the stage with the* PRIOR *at the center. As* MONK NO. 6 *reaches his* D R *position, he genuflects toward the crucifix and then stands facing into the circle. Each monk follows in turn, ending with the last man on the left. When the line is formed,* MARTIN *appears* U L, *wearing a coarse grey loincloth, his hands together in prayer and his head bowed. He solemnly crosses from* L *to* R, *circling behind the monks to* D R *and then across to* C, *where he kneels facing the* PRIOR *and bows head to floor. The light is ghostly, the monks, a row of black columns;* MARTIN, *a pale vulnerable figure in the center. When the* Veni Creator *ends, the* PRIOR *steps forward four paces.*]

PRIOR. Now you must choose one of two ways: Either to leave us now, or give up this world, and devote yourself entirely to God and our Order. But I must add this: Once you have committed yourself, you are not free, for whatever reason, to throw off the yoke of obedience, for you will have accepted it freely, while you were still able to discard it. [*The* CANTOR *sings the Proprio Filio solo.* MARTIN *bows head to floor.* BROTHER WEINAND *crosses to Prior's right with Martin's robes.* MONK NO. 1 *crosses to the Prior's left with the censer, kisses the Prior's hand. The* PRIOR *takes the censer, blesses the robes, hands the censer back to* MONK NO. 1, *who backs into place.* MONK NO. 2 *crosses to the* PRIOR *with the holy water, kisses the Prior's hand. The* PRIOR *takes the twig and blesses the robes, returns the twig to* MONK NO. 2 *who then backs into place. Following the ritual, the* PRIOR *turns to* MARTIN *who kneels up as the Proprio ends.*] He whom it was your will to dress in the garb of the Order, O Lord, invest him also with eternal life. [*The* PRIOR *steps down to* MARTIN, *places his hands over Martin's head.*] The Lord divest you of the former man and of all his works. The Lord invest you with the new man.

[*The choir sings the* Miserere. MONK NO. 5 *and* MONK NO. 6 *move in from* R *and* L *to act as dressers. The* PRIOR *takes the robe from* WEINAND, *holds it out for* MARTIN *to kiss, and the dressers then place it over Martin's head. The scapular follows with the same ceremony, then the hood, and finally the belt.* MARTIN *has been kneeling throughout. While* MARTIN *is tying the belt, the dressers and* BROTHER WEINAND *back into place. The* Miserere *ends and* MONK NO. 4 *crosses to* MARTIN'S *right with the Bible. The* PRIOR *opens the book to the marker.* MARTIN *places his hand on the page and reads the oath.*]

MARTIN. "I, Brother Martin, do make profession and promise obedience to Almighty God, to Mary the Sacred Virgin, and to you, my brother Prior of this cloister, in the name of the Vicar General of the order of Eremites of the holy Bishop of St. Augustine and his successors, to live without property and in chastity according to the Rule of our Venerable Father Augustine until death." [MONK NO. 4 *closes the Bible and backs into place. The* PRIOR *backs into place.* MARTIN *prostrates himself, arms extended. The* PRIOR *and monks turn in unison and kneel, facing the crucifix, crossing themselves.*]

PRIOR. Lord Jesus Christ, our leader and our strength, by the fire of humility you have set aside this servant, Martin, from the rest of mankind. We humbly pray that this fire will also cut him off from carnal intercourse and from the community of those things done on earth by men, through the sanctity shed from Heaven upon him, and that you will bestow on him grace to remain yours, and merit eternal life. For it is

not he who begins, but he who endures will be saved. Amen.
[*On "Amen," all cross themselves and rise, facing* C *with
open books, and sing the "Te Deum."* MARTIN *rises and with
hands together in prayer position, crosses* up *to the Prior,
whom he kisses on both cheeks (right first), and then backs*
D C. *They bow slightly to each other.* MARTIN *crosses to the
monk* D R *and performs the same ritual, stepping back only
two steps as he moves to each monk in turn. After ac-
knowledging Martin's bow and as* MARTIN *passes on to the
next, each monk turns to the crucifix, genuflects, and crosses
up and out* L. MARTIN *skips the Prior but genuflects to the
crucifix as he crosses* C. *When the last monk has received
the kiss of peace,* MARTIN *genuflects to the crucifix and follows* U L *and exits. The* PRIOR *turns upstage, genuflects and
exits last. The singing continues off stage.*]

[*As the* PRIOR *is exiting, two figures appear* D L. *Martin's father* HANS *crosses* U L *and stands looking after the monks.
He is a stocky man, wired throughout with a miner's muscle,
lower-middle class, on his way to becoming a small primi-
tive capitalist; bewildered, full of pride and resentment.*
LUCAS, *his companion, peers about as the eerie lights of the
ceremony fade, and general lighting builds. He genuflects
before the crucifix and kneels for a moment, then rises to
stare at the crucifix. They both carry hats.*]

HANS. Well?

LUCAS. Well?

HANS. Don't "well" me, you feeble old ninny, what do you
think?

LUCAS. Think? Of what?

HANS. Yes, think, man, think. What do you think, pen and
ink, think of all that?

LUCAS. Oh——

HANS. Oh! Of all these monks, of Martin and all the rest of
it? You've been sitting in this arse-aching congregation,
you've been watching, haven't you? What about it?

LUCAS. Yes, well, I must say it's all very impressive.

HANS. Oh, yes?

LUCAS. No getting away from it.

HANS. Impressive?

LUCAS. Deeply. It was so moving—so——

HANS. What?

LUCAS. You must have felt it, surely. You couldn't fail to.

HANS [*crossing* D L]. Impressive! I don't know what impresses me any longer.

LUCAS. Oh, come on——

HANS. Impressive!

LUCAS. Of course it is, and you know it.

HANS [*turning back*]. Oh, it's all right for you—you can afford to be impressed.

LUCAS. Surely it's too late for any regrets, or bitterness, Hans. It obviously must be God's will, and there's an end of it.

HANS [*crossing back to* LUCAS C]. That's exactly what it is— an end of it! Very fine for you, my old friend, very fine indeed. You're just losing a son-in-law, and you can take your pick of plenty more of those where he comes from. But what am I losing? I'm losing a son; mark, a son.

LUCAS. How can you say that?

HANS. How can I say it? I do say it, that's how. [*Crossing* D R.] God's eyes! Two sons to the Plague and now another. Did you see that haircut? Like an egg with a beard.

LUCAS. There isn't a finer order than these people, not the Dominicans or Franciscans. You said that yourself.

HANS. Oh, I suppose they're Christians under their damned cowls.

LUCAS. There are good, distinguished men in this place, and well you know it.

HANS [*crossing* U R]. Yes—good, distinguished men——

LUCAS. Pious, learned men, men from the University like Martin.

HANS. Learned! Some of them can't read their own names.

LUCAS. So?

HANS [*crossing to* LUCAS]. So! I—I'm a miner. I don't need

books. You can't see to read books under the ground. But
Martin's a scholar.

LUCAS. He most certainly is.

HANS. A Master of Arts! What's he master of now? Eh? Tell
me.

LUCAS. Well, there it is. God's gain is your loss. [*Bell strikes
twice.*] We should be going, I suppose.

HANS. Half these monks do nothing but wash dishes and beg
in the streets.

LUCAS. Come on, Hans.

HANS [*turning* R]. He could have been a man of stature.

LUCAS. And he will, with God's help.

HANS. Don't tell me. He could have been a lawyer.

LUCAS. Well, he won't now.

HANS. No, you're damn right he won't. Of stature. To the
Archbishop or the Duke, or——

LUCAS. Yes.

HANS. Anyone.

LUCAS. Come on.

HANS. Anyone you can think of.

LUCAS [*crossing* L]. Well, I'm going.

HANS. Brother Martin!

LUCAS [*turning back*]. Hans.

HANS [*crossing to* C]. Do you know why? Lucas: Why? What
made him do it? [*He has ceased to play a role by this time
and he asks the question simply as if he expected a short,
direct answer.*] What made him do it?

LUCAS [*beckoning*]. Let's go home.

HANS. That's what I can't understand. Why? Why?

LUCAS. Home. Let's go home.

[*Bell chimes.* LUCAS *exits* D L, HANS *follows. The lights fade
on the forestage and build at the back where* MONKS *appear
from* U L *carrying a long table set with wooden mugs and
spoons and a round loaf of black bread. They are followed
by monks carrying two long benches which are set at either
side of the table* U C. *The monk at the right end of the*

table exits D R *and returns with a lectern and book which
he places* U R. *He then stands with hands folded in prayer
waiting for the benediction. The remaining monks file on
to stand at either side of the table. The monk playing the
reader stands at the right end of the table, facing the* PRIOR
at the left end. MARTIN (*who has carried the left end of the
table and then exited for the Prior's chair which he places
just behind the Prior*) *stands just back of the Prior's chair.
When all are in place, the bell stops and the Prior gives the
blessing.*]

PRIOR. *Oremus. Benedic, Domine, nos, et haec tua dona, quae
de tua largitatae sumus sumpturi, Per Christum Dominum
nostrum.*

ALL. Amen.

[*The* MONKS *cross themselves and file to the front of the
benches to sit.* MARTIN *seats the* PRIOR *and exits* D L. *The*
READER *moves to the lectern and commences to read aloud.
The monk who placed the lectern exits* D L *with* MARTIN
*and returns immediately wearing a leather apron and carry-
ing a tray stacked with wooden bowls. He gives one to the*
PRIOR *and then moves to the right end of the table and
bowls are passed along to the seated monks. He then exits*
D L. MARTIN *follows, wearing a leather apron and carrying
a pitcher of wine. He pours for the* PRIOR *and then for each
monk across the back of the table and left across the front.
As he starts to exit* D L, *he is stopped by the words of the*
READER. *He stands and listens, raising his head on "... to
hate your own will." He is startled by the other serving
monk rushing on with tray to collect the bowls and he exits
hurriedly* D L. *He leaves the pitcher offstage and returns to
stand behind the Prior's chair, where he is joined by the
other serving monk when the bowls have been cleared.*]

READER. What are the tools of Good Works?

First, to love Lord God with all one's heart, all one's soul,
and all one's strength. Then, one's neighbor as oneself. Then,
not to kill.

Not to commit adultery
Not to steal
Not to covet
Not to bear false witness
To honor all men
To deny yourself, in order to follow Christ
To chastise the body
Not to seek soft living
To love fasting
To clothe the naked
To visit the sick
To bury the dead
To prefer nothing to the love of Christ.

Not to yield to anger
Not to nurse a grudge
Not to hold guile in your heart
Not to make a feigned peace
To fear the Day of Judgment
To dread Hell
To desire eternal life with all your spiritual longing
To keep death daily before your eyes
To keep constant vigilance over the actions of your life
To know for certain that God sees you everywhere
When evil thoughts come into your heart, to dash them at
once on the love of Christ
To apply yourself frequently to prayer
Daily in your prayer, with tears and signs to confess your
past sins to God
Not to fulfill the desires of the flesh
To hate your own will.

Behold, these are the tools of the spiritual craft. If we em-
ploy these unceasingly day and night, and render account of
them on the Day of Judgment, then we shall receive from
the Lord in return that reward that He Himself has promised: Eye hath not seen nor ear heard what God hath prepared for those that love Him. Now this is the workshop in

which we shall diligently execute all these tasks. May God
grant that you observe all these rules cheerfully as lovers of
spiritual beauty, spreading around you by the piety of your
deportment the sweet odor of Christ. [*As the* READER *fin-
ishes, bell chimes four times. The monks rise from the table,
file to the outside of the benches and bow heads for the
prayer.*]

PRIOR. *Agimus tibi gratias, omnipotens Deus, pro universis
beneficiis tuis; qui vivis et regnas in saecula saeculorum.*
ALL. Amen. [*They cross themselves.*]

[*Bell chimes four times. On the fourth chime, the organ commences and continues into the confession scene, fading as
indicated below. The upstage lights fade as the monks remove the benches and table off* U L. MARTIN *removes the
Prior's chair and returns for the left end of the table. The*
READER *takes the lectern off* D R *and picks up a chair for
the Prior which he places* D R *facing on stage. The* PRIOR
*takes position standing in front of the chair. The monks
form a double line across the stage facing the Prior. The*
PRIOR *is lit from above, the monks from the wing* D R
*straight across the stage. The crucifix is illuminated from a
low angle off* U L. *When the line is formed, the bell chimes
once. All monks kneel in place.*]

PRIOR. *Ave, Maria, gratia plena; Dominus tecum: benedicta tu
in mulieribus, et benedictus fructus ventris tui Jesus.*
ALL [*joining* PRIOR]. *Sancta Maria, Mater Dei, ora pro nobis
peccatoribus, nunc et in hora mortis nostrae.* Amen.

[*The* PRIOR *sits. Monks kneel back on heels, heads bowed,
hands folded under scapulars. During the above prayer, the
serving monk rushes in and joins the line, followed by* MAR-
TIN *who kneels alone at the end of the line.* MARTIN'S *lines
during the confessions are spoken thoughts and not acknowl-
edged by the confessing monks or* PRIOR *until the final open
confession which* MARTIN *makes formally and kneeling up.
When each monk confesses, he kneels up facing the Prior,*

and chants the confession on one note, dropping a tone on the last syllable. He strikes his chest with his right hand at the start and end of his speech.]

WEINAND. I confess to God, to Blessed Mary and our holy Father Augustine, to all saints, and to all present, that I have sinned exceedingly in thought, word, and deed by my own fault.

MONK NO. 8. I confess I did leave my cell for the Night Office without scapular and had to return for it. For this failure to Christ I abjectly seek forgiveness and whatever punishment the Prior and community is pleased to impose on me.

MARTIN [*not chanting*]. I am a worm and no man, a byword and a laughingstock.

MONK NO. 1. I confess. I did omit to have a candle ready at the mass.

MONK NO. 6. Twice in my sloth, I have omitted to shave, and even excused myself, pretending to believe my skin to be fairer than that of my brothers.

MARTIN. Crush me out the worminess in me, stamp on me.

MONK NO. 3. I confess I did ask for a bath, pretending to myself that it was necessary for my health, but as I lowered my body into the tub, it came to me that it was an inordinate desire and that it was my soul that was soiled.

MARTIN [*lit by a special light in the foots so that his shadow is large on the back wall, he examines his hands as he crouches low at the end of the line*]. If my flesh would leak and dissolve, and I could live as bone, if I were all bone, plucked bone and brain, warm hair and a bony heart, if I were all bone, I could brandish myself without terror, without any terror at all—I could be indestructible.

MONK NO. 2. Let Brother Paulinus remember our visit to our near sister house, and lifting his eyes repeatedly at a woman in the town who dropped alms into his bag.

MONK NO. 9. I remember, and I beg forgiveness.

PRIOR. Then let him remember also that though our dear

Father Augustine does not forbid us to see women, he blames us if we should desire them.

MARTIN. My bones fail. My bones fail, my bones are shattered and fall away, my bones fail and all that's left of me is a scraped marrow and a dying jelly.

MONK NO. 10. I confess I have three times made mistakes in the Oratory, psalm singing and Antiphon.

MONK NO. 4. Let Brother Norbert also remember his breakage while working in the kitchen.

MONK NO. 10. I remember it, and confess humbly.

PRIOR. Let him remember also his greater transgression in not coming at once to his Prior and community to do penance for it.

MARTIN. I am alone, I am alone, and against myself.

MONK NO. 10. I confess it. I confess it, and beg your prayers that I may undergo the greater punishment for it.

PRIOR. Take heart, you shall be punished, and severely.

MONK NO. 8. I confess that while bottling wine . . . [*Stopping as drowned out by following, glares at* MARTIN *and kneels back.*]

MARTIN [*kneels up, cutting in on speech above with fervently chanted confession*]. I confess that I have offended grievously against humility, being sometimes discontented with the meanest and worst of everything. Not only have I failed to declare myself to myself lower and lower and of less account than all other men, but I have failed in my most inmost heart to believe it. For many weeks, many weeks it seemed to me, I was put to cleaning the latrines. I did it vigorously, not tepidly, with all my poor strength, without whispering or objections to anyone. But although I fulfilled my task, and I did it well, sometimes there were murmurings in my heart. I prayed that they would cease, knowing that God, seeing my murmuring heart, must reject my work, and it was as good as not done. I sought out my master, and he told me to fast for two days. I have fasted for three, but, even so, I can't tell if the murmurings are really gone, and

I ask for your prayers, and I ask for your prayers that I may be able to go on fulfilling the same task.

PRIOR. Let Brother Martin remember all the degrees of humility; and let him go on cleaning the latrines. [*Bell chimes once. All kneel with heads to the floor.* PRIOR *stands. Bell chimes again, all kneel up. During the following prayer, the prior makes the sign of the cross over the kneeling monks and they bless themselves simultaneously and in the same rhythm.*]

PRIOR. *Indulgentiam, absolutionem et remissionem peccatorum nostrorum tribuat nobis omnipotens et misericors Dominus.*

ALL. Amen.

[*Bell chimes four times or until the choir has assembled. The confession lights fade as light upstage builds. The monks assemble in a triangle facing upstage, with the* PRIOR *at the head directly under the crucifix, with four monks, backs to the audience, in the downstage row.* MARTIN *is in their midst. Led by the cantor they all sing "Deus in Adjutorium." Presently there is a quiet moaning, just distinguishable amongst the voices. It becomes louder and wilder and there is some confusion in Martin's section of the choir. The singing goes right on and only a few heads turn furtively as* MARTIN *emerges in a rigid stagger. His body seems to be stiffening, the arms held forward from the body and fists and jaw clenched. He makes a frantic effort to speak and eventually he is able to roar out a word at a time.*]

MARTIN. Not! Me! I am not!

[*The attack reaches its height, the jaw clenches, foam appears at the corner of the mouth, the eyes roll back and the body falls stiffly backward, head to stage* R. *On striking the floor, the arms and legs flail, and groaning increases through the clenched teeth.* BROTHER WEINAND, *who is at the right end of the back line, and the monk next to him rush to help, each taking an arm. A third monk from the back line joins them, and holds Martin's legs still.* WEINAND *pins Martin's arm under his knee, takes his head in his lap and pries open the clenched jaw.* MARTIN *gives a great gasp, the tension is released and the fit is over.* WEINAND *and one monk each take an arm and hoist* MARTIN *to his feet, then with his arms over their shoulders they drag him off* D L *as he gasps for air and seems about to vomit. The remaining monk returns to his place in line. The Office has continued as if nothing had taken place. As the lights fade,* WEINAND *and his companion return to the line. As the singing ends with "sedea dextris meis" the bell chimes twice. The stage fades to black-out and the choir disperses.*]

CURTAIN

ACT ONE

Scene Two

It is a year later. As the chimes fade from the previous scene, a throbbing melody from a solo cello fills the darkness. In a pinpoint of light D C *we see* MARTIN'S *face appear, pale, perspiring, and tousled, as though suddenly wakened from a terrifying nightmare. The cello fades down, but continues through the speech.*]

MARTIN. I lost the body of a child, a child's body, the eyes of a child; and at the first sound of my own childish voice. I lost the body of a child; and I was afraid, and I went back to find it. But I'm still afraid. I'm afraid, and there's an end of it! But I mean . . . continually! For instance, of the noise the Prior's dog makes on a still evening when he rolls over on his side and licks his teeth. [*As the speech continues, the giant crucifix behind* MARTIN *is gradually illumi-*

nated from two sides, casting grotesque shadows across the entire back wall. MARTIN *continues, unaware of the apparition behind him.*] I'm afraid of the darkness, and the hole in it; and I see it some time of every day! And some days more than once even, and there's no bottom to it. Why? Why, do you think? The lost body of a child, hanging on a mother's tit, and close to the big, warm body of a man, and I can't find it!

[*As* MARTIN *nears the end of the speech the cello swells. He seems to sense the agonized image behind him; he whirls, cries out and flings himself into the shadows* D R. *He is kneeling, hunched, trying to pray when Brother Weinand's calls from off* L *seem to bring him out of his nightmare. The apparition fades, lights around* MARTIN *build.*]

WEINAND [*off* L, *approaching*]. Brother Martin! Brother Martin!

[BROTHER WEINAND *enters* U L.]

WEINAND. Brother Martin!

MARTIN. Yes.

WEINAND [*crossing* D R]. Oh, Brother Martin. Your father's here.

MARTIN. My father?

WEINAND. He asked to see you, but I told him it'd be better to wait until afterwards.

MARTIN. Where is he?

WEINAND. He's having breakfast with the Prior.

MARTIN. Is he alone?

WEINAND. No.

MARTIN. Is my mother with him?

WEINAND. No.

MARTIN. What did he have to come for? I should have told him not to come.

WEINAND. It'd be a strange father who didn't want to be present when his son celebrated his first Mass.

MARTIN. I never thought he'd come. Why didn't he tell me?

WEINAND. Well, he's here now anyway. He's also given twenty guilden to the chapter as a present, so he can't be too displeased with you.

MARTIN. Twenty guilden.

WEINAND. Well, are you all prepared?

MARTIN [*turning to face* WEINAND]. That's more than three times what it cost him to send me to the University for a year.

WEINAND. You don't look it. Why, you're running all over with sweat again. Are you sick?

MARTIN. No.

WEINAND [*pulling* MARTIN *to his feet*]. Are you?

MARTIN. No.

WEINAND. Here, let me wipe your face. [*Takes handkerchief from belt and mops Martin's brow and right cheek.*] You haven't much time. You're sure you're not sick?

MARTIN. My bowels won't move, that's all. But that's nothing out of the way.

WEINAND [*stops mopping*]. Have you shaved?

MARTIN. Yes. Before I went to confession. Why, do you think I should shave again?

WEINAND. No. I don't. A few overlooked little bristles couldn't make much difference any more than a few imaginary sins. [*Mopping.*] There, that's better.

MARTIN. What do you mean?

WEINAND. You were sweating like a pig in a butcher's shop. You know what they say, don't you? Wherever you find a melancholy spirit, there you'll find a bath running for the devil.

MARTIN. No, no, what did you mean about leaving a few imaginary sins?

WEINAND. I mean there are plenty of priests with dirty ears administering the sacraments, but this isn't the time to talk about that. Come on, Martin, you've got nothing to be afraid of.

MARTIN. How do you know?

WEINAND. You always talk as though lightning were just about to strike behind you.

MARTIN. Tell me what you meant.

WEINAND. I only meant the whole convent knows you're always making up sins you've never committed.

MARTIN [*turning away*]. What's the use of all this talk of penitence if I can't feel it?

WEINAND. The moment you've confessed and turned to the altar, you're beckoning for a priest again. Why, every time you break wind they say you rush to a confessor.

MARTIN. Do they say that?

WEINAND. It's their favorite joke.

MARTIN. They say that, do they?

WEINAND. Martin! You're protected from many of the world's evils in here. You're expected to master them, not be obsessed by them. God bids us hope in His everlasting mercy. Try to remember that.

MARTIN [*crossing* L *above* WEINAND *to* L C]. And you tell me this! What have I gained from coming into this sacred order? Aren't I still the same? I'm still envious, I'm still impatient, I'm still passionate?

WEINAND. How can you ask a question like that?

MARTIN. I do ask it. I'm asking you now! What have I gained?

WEINAND. In any of this, all we can ever learn is how to die.

MARTIN. That's no answer.

WEINAND. It's the only one I can think of at this moment. [*Crosses to* C.] Come on, man.

MARTIN. All you can teach me in this sacred place is how to doubt——

WEINAND. Give you a little praise, and you're pleased for a while, but let a little trial of sin and death come into your day and you crumble, don't you?

MARTIN. But that's all you've taught me, that's really all you've taught me, and all the while I'm living in the Devil's wormbag.

WEINAND [*out of patience*]. *Martin!* [*Crossing to take* MARTIN

by the shoulders.] It hurts me to see you like this, sucking
up cares like a leech.

MARTIN. You *will* be there beside me, won't you?

WEINAND. Of course, and, if anything at all goes wrong, or if
you forget anything, we'll see to it. But nothing will. You'll
be all right. You won't make any mistakes.

MARTIN. But what if I do, just one mistake, one word—one
sin.

WEINAND. Martin, kneel down. [*Kneeling, drawing* MARTIN
down.]

MARTIN. Forgive me, Brother Weinand, but the truth is
this——

WEINAND. Kneel. [MARTIN *kneels; their hands are clasped together.*]

MARTIN. It's this, just this. All I can feel is God's hatred.

WEINAND. Repeat the Apostles' Creed.

MARTIN. He's like a glutton, the way he gorges me, he's a
glutton. He gorges me, and then spits me out in lumps.

WEINAND. After me. "I believe in God the Father Almighty,
maker of Heaven and Earth . . ."

MARTIN. I'm a trough, I tell you, and he's swilling about in
me. All the time.

WEINAND. "And in Jesus Christ, His only Son Our Lord . . ."

MARTIN. "And in Jesus Christ, His only Son Our Lord . . ."

WEINAND. "Who was conceived by the Holy Ghost, born of
the Virgin Mary, suffered under Pontius Pilate . . ."

MARTIN [*almost unintelligibly*]. "Was crucified, dead and
buried; He descended into Hell, the third day He rose
from the dead, He ascended into Heaven, and sitteth on the
right hand of God the Father Almighty; from thence He
shall come to judge the living and the dead." And every
sunrise sings a song of death.

WEINAND. "I believe——"

MARTIN. "I believe——"

WEINAND. Go on.

MARTIN. "I believe in the Holy Ghost; the holy Catholic
Church; the Communion of Saints; the forgiveness of sins;"

WEINAND. Again!

MARTIN. "The forgiveness of sins."

WEINAND. What was that again?

MARTIN. "I believe in the forgiveness of sins."

WEINAND. Do you? Do you? Then remember this: St. Bernard says that when we say in the Apostles' Creed, "I believe in the forgiveness of sins," each one must believe that *his* sins are forgiven. [MARTIN *seems to relax, slumps back on heels.*] Well?

MARTIN [*turning downstage*]. I wish my bowels would open. I'm blocked up like an old crypt.

[MONKS NO. 5 *and* 6 *enter* U R *carrying a litter with the folded mass vestments which they place* R C. *They are followed by six monks* (NOS. 1, 2, 3, 8, 9, 10) *who stand in groups* U R.]

WEINAND. Try to remember, Martin?

MARTIN. Yes, I'll try.

WEINAND [*rising*]. Good. Now, you must get yourself ready. Come on, we'd better help you. [*He helps* MARTIN, *who staggers a bit on rising but quickly collects himself and crosses* R *to the waiting dressers. First the amice is placed over his head.* MARTIN *guides the tie strings across his chest and the dresser ties them at his back.* MARTIN *is perspiring and mops his brow.* BROTHER WEINAND *crosses to him, hands him a handkerchief, and steps back toward* C. *The dressers then hold the white alb in front of* MARTIN. *He puts his arms through the sleeves and they tie the alb down the back. During this business* WEINAND *has crossed back of the group to the litter, picked up the stole and moved* D R, *watching the dressing.*]

MARTIN. How much did you say my father gave to the chapter?

WEINAND. Twenty guilden.

MARTIN. That's a lot of money to my father. He's a miner, you know.

WEINAND. Yes, he told me.

MARTIN. As tough as you can think of. Where's he sitting?

WEINAND. Near the front, I should think. [*Bell chimes four times. The six monks upstage form a line facing* L *and led by the cantor. After the fourth chime, the cantor starts the "Exultet," singing the first line solo; the others then join and the procession starts slowly off* L. *During this* WEINAND *has held out the stole for* MARTIN *to kiss, then places it around his neck. It is crossed in front and anchored with the white cord belt which the dressers are tying. They then place the chasuble over Martin's head and adjust it to be straight front and back.* WEINAND *again crosses behind, picking up the maniple en route* D C. *When the chasuble is straightened, the dressers pull the amice back off Martin's head forming a collar which is partially tucked under the chasuble. When finished, the dressers step back and* WEINAND *dismisses them with a nod. They pick up the litter and exit* U R. MARTIN *turns to* WEINAND, *who hands him the maniple to kiss and then places it over Martin's left wrist and steps back to inspect* MARTIN, *who is now ready for mass.*]

MARTIN. Thank you, Brother Weinand.

WEINAND. For what? Today would be an ordeal for any kind of man. In a short while, you will be handling, for the first time, the body and blood of Christ. God bless you, my son. [WEINAND *blesses* MARTIN, *who crosses himself.* WEINAND *starts to exit* U L *after the procession but* MARTIN *stops him.*]

MARTIN. Somewhere, in the body of a child, Satan foresaw in me what I'm suffering now. That's why he prepares all kinds of tricks for me, so that I keep wondering if I'm the only man living who's baited, and surrounded by dreams.

WEINAND [*losing patience, really angry now, crosses a few steps back to* MARTIN]. You're a fool. You're really a fool. God isn't angry with you. It's you who are angry with Him. [*Bell chimes twice. The "Exultet," which has continued off-stage, ends here.* BROTHER WEINAND *exits rapidly* U L.]

[MONK NO. 4 *enters* U R *with a crucifix on a tall staff. Behind him enter the dressers* (MONKS NO. 5 *and* NO. 6) *with large lighted candles. They stand waiting for* MARTIN, *who turns away from* WEINAND *and kneels downstage.*]

MARTIN. Oh, Mary, dear Mary, all I see of Christ is a flame and raging on a rainbow. Pray to your Son, and ask Him to still His anger, for I can't raise my eyes to look at Him. Am I the only one to see all this, and suffer? [*The "Kyrie" is heard off* L. MARTIN, *still kneeling, turns his head, startled and anxious; he rises and crosses up to join the procession between the crucifix and the candlemen. At a nod from* MARTIN *the monk with the crucifix starts across,* MARTIN *and the candlemen following.* MARTIN *stops briefly halfway across. The crucifix goes right on. The candlemen hold. Then* MARTIN *gathers his courage and continues off* L, *hands together in prayer.*]

[*The* KNIGHT *enters* D R *as* MARTIN *is crossing the stage, he watches* MARTIN *off from* U C, *then crosses down to center stage with one light remaining directly down on him from overhead.*]

KNIGHT. And so, the praising ended—and the blasphemy began.

[*The light blacks out. The "Kyrie" swells to a conclusion in the dark and ends. There is a pause and we hear monkish laughter off* L *as the lights start to build for the next scene.*]

ACT ONE

Scene Three

SCENE: *The convent refectory. As the light builds, a group enters from* U L, *chuckling and in a party mood.* WEINAND *leads, followed by* MONK NO. 1 *carrying a pitcher of wine, then* HANS, *who carries his hat and is draining the dregs of a mug.* LUCAS *is with them.* MONKS NO. 2 *and* NO. 4 *carry*

the table which has two benches on top of it, MONK NO. 9
follows with a stool. MONK NO. 6 *carries a mug and* MONK
NO. 10 *follows with a tray with five mugs upside down on
it. Wine has warmed* HANS *and he is in a boisterous mood.
During the dialogue the table is placed* D L *and the benches
lifted off and placed at each side. The stool is placed at the
left end of the table. The monk with the tray passes mugs to*
MONKS NO. 1, NO. 4 *and* NO. 9, *places one on the table
which Weinand will use for Martin later, and stands waiting* D L *with one mug remaining.*]

WEINAND [*crossing* R C]. This way, please. . . .

HANS [*following to* C]. What about some more of this, eh?
Don't think you can get away with it, you know, you old
cockchafer. I'm getting me twenty guildens' worth before
the day's out. After all, it's a proud day for all of us. That's
right, isn't it?

LUCAS [*crossing* D L]. It certainly is.

WEINAND. Forgive me, I wasn't looking. Here—— [*He fills*
HANS' *mug.*]

HANS [*trying to be friendly*]. Don't give me that. You monks
don't miss much. Got eyes like gimlets and ears like open
drains. Tell me—come on, then, what's your opinion of
Brother Martin?

WEINAND. He's a good, devout monk. [*Pouring for the monk
at his right.*]

HANS [*crossing to sit above right end of table*]. Yes. Yes, well,
I suppose you can't say much about each other, can you?
You're more like a team, in a way. Tell me, Brother—
would you say that in this monastery—or, any monastery
you like—you were as strong as the weakest member of the
team?

WEINAND. No, I don't think that's so. [*Crossing* L *to pour
for* LUCAS *at stool, then pours for monks above table.*]

HANS. But wouldn't you say then—I'm not saying this in any
criticism, mind, but because I'm naturally interested, in the

circumstances—but wouldn't you say that one bad monk, say
for instance one monster-sized, roaring great bitch of a
monk, if he got going, really going, I mean, couldn't he get
his order such a reputation that eventually, it might even
have to go into—what do they call it now—liquidation.
That's it. Liquidation. Now, you're an educated man, you
understand Latin and Greek and Hebrew——

[MONK NO. 5 *enters* D L *with bread, cheese and fruit.*]

WEINAND [*crossing down to center of table*]. Only Latin, I'm
afraid, and very little Greek.

HANS [*having planted his cue for a quick, innocent boast*].
Oh, really. Martin knows Latin and Greek, and now he's
half-way through Hebrew too, they tell me.

WEINAND [*crossing* D L, *takes mug from* MONK NO. 10, *gives
him pitcher and sends him off for refill*]. Martin is a brilliant man. We are not all as gifted as he is. [MONK NO. 5
places food on table and crosses R *to join* MONK NO. 2.]

HANS. No, well, anyway, what would be your opinion about
this?

WEINAND. I think my opinion would be that the Church is bigger than those who are in her. [MONKS NO. 6 *and* NO. 4
cross down to table for food.]

HANS. Yes, yes, but don't you think it could be discredited by,
say, just a few men?

WEINAND. Plenty of people have tried, but the Church is still
there. Besides, a human voice is small and the world's very
large. But the Church reaches out and is heard everywhere.

HANS [*rising, crossing* D C]. Well, what about this chap Erasmus, for instance?

WEINAND [*politely; he knows* HANS *knows nothing about
him*]. Yes?

HANS. Erasmus. [*Trying to pass the ball.*] Well, what about
him, for instance? What do you think about him?

WEINAND. Erasmus is apparently a great scholar, and respected
throughout Europe.

HANS [*resenting being lectured*]. Yes, of course, *I* know who

he is, I don't need you to tell me that. What I said was:
What do you think about him?

WEINAND. Think about him?

HANS. Good God, you won't stand still a minute and let yourself be saddled, will you? Doesn't he criticize the Church or
something?

WEINAND. He's a scholar, and, I should say, his criticisms
could best be argued about by other scholars.

[MONK NO. 10 *returns with refilled pitcher and exchanges it
for mug* WEINAND *holds.*]

LUCAS. Don't let him get you into an argument. He'll argue
about anything, especially if he doesn't know what he's talking about.

HANS. I know what I'm talking about, I was merely asking a
question——

LUCAS [*rising from stool, and sitting front bench*]. Well, you
shouldn't be asking questions on a day like today. Just think
of it, for a minute, Hans——

HANS. What do you think I'm doing? You soppy old woman!
[MONK NO. 4 *passes fruit to* MONKS NO. 5 *and* NO. 2 D R.]

LUCAS. It's a really "once only" occasion, like a wedding, if
you like.

HANS [*turning to monks* R]. Or a funeral. By the way, what's
happened to the corpse? Eh? Where's Brother Martin?
[MONK NO. 5 *evades* HANS *by taking fruit left to* MONK
NO. 10.]

WEINAND. I expect he's still in his cell.

HANS. Well, what's he doing in there?

WEINAND. He's perfectly all right, he's a little—disturbed.

HANS [*pouncing delightedly*]. Disturbed! Disturbed. What's
he disturbed about?

WEINAND [*crossing to above* C *table, pouring for* MONK NO. 6
who is seated]. Celebrating one's first Mass can be a great
ordeal for a sensitive spirit.

HANS. Oh, the bread and the wine and all that?

WEINAND. Of course; there are a great many things to memorize as well. [MONKS NO. 2 *and* NO. 4 *cross* L *to above table where* WEINAND *refills mugs.*]

LUCAS. Heavens, yes. I don't know how they think of it all.

HANS. I didn't think he made it up as he went along!

LUCAS. The boy's probably a bit—well, you know, anxious about seeing you again, too.

HANS. What's he got to be anxious about?

LUCAS. Well, apart from anything else, it's nearly three years since he last saw you.

HANS. I saw *him*. He didn't see me.

[MARTIN, *pale, tentative, anxious, enters* U R, *crossing* D R. LUCAS *sees him first, then* WEINAND *and the monks.* HANS *turns but says nothing.*]

LUCAS [*rising, crossing to* MARTIN *to save awkward situation*]. There you are, my boy. We were wondering what had happened to you. Come and sit down, there's a good lad. Your father and I have been punishing the convent wine cellar, I'm afraid. Bit early in the day for me, too.

HANS [*turning* R]. Speak for yourself, you swirly-eyed old gander. We're not *started* yet, are we?

LUCAS. My dear boy, are you all right? You're so pale. [MONK NO. 5 *returns fruit tray to table and sits above;* MONK NO. 10 *sits on stool* L.]

HANS. He's right, though. Brother Martin! Brother Lazarus they ought to call you! [*He laughs and* MARTIN *smiles at the joke with him.* MARTIN *is cautious,* HANS *too, but maneuvering for position.*]

MARTIN. I'm all right, thank you, Lucas.

HANS. Been sick, have you?

MARTIN. I'm much better now, thank you, Father.

HANS [*relentlessly*]. Upset tummy, is it? That what it is? Too much fasting, I expect. [*Concealing concern.*] You look like death warmed up, all right.

LUCAS. Come and have a little wine. You're allowed that, aren't you? It'll make you feel better. [WEINAND *picks up mug from table, crosses with pitcher to* MARTIN, *hands him mug and pours for him.* MARTIN *drinks immediately.*]

HANS. I know that milky look. I've seen it too many times. Been sick, have you?

LUCAS. Oh, he's looking better already. Drop of wine'll put the color back in there. You're all right, aren't you, lad?

MARTIN. Yes, what about you——

LUCAS. That's right. Of course he is. He's all right.

HANS. Vomit all over your cell, I expect. [*Crossing above table to monks on bench.*] But he'll have to clear that up himself, won't he?

LUCAS [*to* MARTIN]. Oh, you weren't, were you? Poor old lad, well, never mind, no wonder you kept us waiting.

HANS. Can't have his mother coming in and getting down on her knees to mop it all up.

MARTIN. I managed to clean it up all right. How are *you,* Father?

HANS [*feeling an attack, but determined not to lose the initiative; crossing* C *and to* MARTIN]. Me? Oh, I'm all right. I'm all right, aren't I, Lucas? Nothing ever wrong with me. Your old man's strong enough. But then that's because we've got to be, people like Lucas and me. Because if *we* aren't strong, it won't take any time at all before we're knocked flat on our backs, or flat on our knees, or flat on something or other. Flat on our backs and finished, and we can't afford to be finished because if we're finished, that's it, that's the end, so we just have to stand up to it as best we can. [*Turns to sit right end of downstage bench.*] But that's life, isn't it?

MARTIN. I'm never sure what people mean when they say that.

LUCAS. Your father's doing very well indeed, Martin. He's got his own investment in the mine now, so he's beginning to work for himself, if you see what I mean. That's the way things are going everywhere now.

MARTIN [*to* HANS]. You must be pleased.

HANS. I'm pleased to make money. I'm not pleased to break my back doing it.

MARTIN. How's Mother?

HANS. Nothing wrong there, either. Too much work and too many kids for too long, that's all. [*Hiding embarrassment.*] I'm sorry she couldn't come, but it's a rotten journey as you know, and all that, so she sent her love to you. Oh, yes, and there was a pie, too. But I was told—[*At* BROTHER WEINAND *who leaves Martin's side and crosses to monk above table.*]—I couldn't give it to you, but I'd have to give it to the Prior.

MARTIN. That's the rule about gifts, Father. You must have forgotten?

HANS. Well, I hope you get a piece of it, anyway. She took a lot of care over it. Oh, yes, and then there was Lucas's girl, she asked to be remembered to you.

MARTIN [*turning to* LUCAS *on his right*]. Oh, good. How is she?

HANS. Didn't she, Lucas? She asked specially to be remembered to Martin, didn't she?

LUCAS. Oh, she often talks about you, Martin. Even now. She's married, you know.

MARTIN. No, I didn't know.

LUCAS. Oh, yes, got two children, one boy and a girl.

HANS. That's it—two on show on the stall, and now another one coming out from under the counter again—right, Lucas?

LUCAS. Yes. Oh, she makes a fine mother.

HANS [*rising, crossing to* MARTIN]. And what's better than that? There's only one way of going "up you" to Old Nick when he does come for you and that's when you show him your kids. It's the one thing—that is, if you've been lucky, and the plagues kept away from you—you can spring it out from under the counter at him. *That* to you! Then you've done something for yourself forever—forever and ever. Amen. [*Blessing all monks at his left. Pause.*] Come along, Brother Martin, don't let your guests go without. Poor old Lucas is standing there with a glass as empty as a nun's womb——

MARTIN. I'm sorry, Lucas.

HANS. —aren't you, you thirsty little goosey? [HANS *moves* R *as* MARTIN *takes* LUCAS *to right end of table, refills mug and sets pitcher down.* LUCAS *sits on upstage bench;* WEINAND *sits and serves cheese and fruit.*] That's right, and don't forget your old dad. [MARTIN *crosses* R *to* HANS, *fills mug and returns to right end of table.*] Yes, well, as I say, I'm sorry your mother couldn't come but I don't suppose she'd have enjoyed it much, although I dare say she'd like to have watched her son perform the Holy Office. Isn't a mother supposed to dance with her son after the ceremony? Like Christ danced with *his* mother? Well, I can't see her doing that. I suppose you think *I'm* going to dance with you instead.

MARTIN. You're not obliged to, Father. [*They have been avoiding any direct contact until now, but now they look at each other, and both relax a little.*]

HANS [*encouraged*]. God's eyes! Come to think of it, you look like a woman, in all that!

MARTIN [*with affection*]. Not any woman you'd want, Father.

HANS. What do you know about it, eh? What do you know about it? [*He laughs but not long.*] Well, Brother Martin.

MARTIN. Well? [*Pause. He crosses* L *above table.*] Would you like some fish? Or a roast, how about that, that's what you'd like, isn't it?

HANS [*stopping* MARTIN *with attack, then crossing* U R, *circling across toward* MARTIN *during speech*]. Brother Martin, old Brother Martin. Well, Brother Martin, you had a right old time up there by that altar for a bit, didn't you? I wouldn't have been in your shoes, I'll tell you. All those people listening to you, every word you're saying, watching every little tiny movement, watching for one little lousy mistake. [BROTHER WEINAND *rises from bench and takes stand beside* MARTIN.] I couldn't keep my eyes off it. We all thought you were going to flunk it for one minute there, didn't we, Lucas?

LUCAS. Well, we did have a few anxious moments——

HANS. Anxious moments! I'll say we did, I thought to myself, "he's going to flunk it, he can't get through it, he's going

to flunk it." What was that bit, you know, the worst bit
where you stopped and Brother——

MARTIN. Weinand.

HANS. Weinand, yes, and he very kindly helped you up. He
was actually holding you up at one point, wasn't he?

MARTIN. Yes.

WEINAND [*stepping between* MARTIN *and* HANS]. It happens
often enough when a young priest celebrates Mass for the
first time.

HANS [*brushing* WEINAND *aside*—WEINAND *crosses slowly to
far* R]. Looked as though he didn't know if it was Christ-
mas or Wednesday. We thought the whole thing had come
to a standstill for a bit, didn't we? Everyone waiting and
nothing happening. What was that bit, Martin, what was it?

MARTIN. I don't remember.

HANS. Yes, you know, the bit you really flunked.

MARTIN [*rattling it off*]. "Receive, O Holy Father, almighty
and eternal God, this spotless host, which I, thine unworthy
servant, offer unto thee for my own innumerable sins of
commission and omission, and for all here present and all
faithful Christians, living and dead, so that it may avail for
their salvation and everlasting life." [HANS *starts to pat* MAR-
TIN'S *shoulder approvingly but* MARTIN, *unable to accept
praise, moves quickly* D L *and crosses to* U C.] When I entered the monastery, I wanted to speak to God directly, you
see, without any embarrassment; I wanted to speak to him
· myself, but when it came to it, I dried up, as I always have.

LUCAS [*rising to join* MARTIN C]. No, you didn't, Martin, it
was only for a few moments. Besides——

MARTIN. Thanks to Brother Weinand. [*Stepping down for a
clear line on* HANS.] Father, why do you hate me being
here? [HANS *is outraged at a direct question.*]

HANS. Eh? What do you mean? I don't hate you being here.

MARTIN. Try to give me a straight answer if you can, Father.
I should like you to tell me.

HANS. What are you talking about, Brother Martin? You don't

know what you're talking about. You've not had enough
wine, that's your trouble.

MARTIN. And don't say I could have been a lawyer.

HANS. Well, so you could have been. You could have been
better than that. You could have been a burgomaster, you
could have been a magistrate, you could have been a chancellor, you could have been anything! I don't want to talk
about it. Anyway, I certainly don't want to talk about it in
front of complete strangers.

MARTIN. You make me sick.

HANS [*sitting on stool at left end of table*]. Oh, do I? Well,
thank you for that, Brother Martin! Thank you for the
truth, anyway.

MARTIN [*at right end of table*]. No, it isn't the truth, it isn't
the truth at all. You're drinking too much wine—and
I'm . . .

HANS. Drinking too much wine! I could drink this convent
piss from here till Gabriel's horn—[MARTIN *turns away,
crosses* R *to* WEINAND *in despair.*]—and from all accounts
that'll blow about next Thursday—so what's the difference?
[*Pause.* HANS *drinks.*] Is this the wine you use? Is it? Well?
I'm asking a straight question myself now. Is this the wine
you use?

MARTIN. Yes.

HANS. Here, have some. [MARTIN *crosses to above table* C. *He
takes it and drinks, puts mug down.*] You know what they
say?

MARTIN. No, what do they say?

HANS. I'll tell you:

> Bread thou art and wine thou art
> And always shall remain so.

[*Monks gasp, and draw back; some bless themselves.*]

MARTIN [*stricken, staring down at* HANS]. My father didn't
mean that. He's a very devout man, I know. [BROTHER
WEINAND *crosses above table and* D L, *quietly dismissing
monks, who exit* U L *and* D L; *then nods to* MARTIN *that*

LUCAS *remains* U C. MARTIN *turns to* LUCAS.] Brother Weinand will show you over the convent. If you've finished,
that is.

LUCAS [*crossing to table, placing mug down, then crossing* D L
to WEINAND]. Yes, oh, yes, I'd like that. Yes, I've had more
than enough, thank you. Right, well, let's go, shall we,
Brother Weinand? I'll come back for you, shall I, Hans,
you'll stay here?

HANS. Just as you like.

LUCAS [*to* MARTIN]. You're looking a bit better now, lad.
Good-by, my boy, but I'll see you before I go, won't I?

MARTIN. Yes, of course. [WEINAND *and* LUCAS *go, leaving*
MARTIN *and* HANS *alone together at either end of table.*]

HANS. Martin, I didn't mean to embarrass you.

MARTIN. No, it was my fault.

HANS. Not in front of everyone.

MARTIN. I shouldn't have asked you a question like that. It was
a shock to see you suddenly. I'd almost forgotten what your
voice sounded like.

HANS. Tell me, son—what made you get all snarled up like
that in the Mass?

MARTIN. You're disappointed, aren't you?

HANS. I simply want to know, that's all. Men like you don't
just forget their words!

MARTIN. I don't understand what happened. I lifted up my
head at the host, and, as I was speaking the words, I heard
. them as if it were the first time, and suddenly—[*Pause.*]
—they struck at my life.

HANS. I don't know. I really don't. Perhaps your father and
mother are wrong, and God's right, after all. Perhaps. Whatever it is you've got to find, you could only find out by becoming a monk; maybe that's the answer.

MARTIN. But you don't believe that. Do you?

HANS. No, no, I don't.

MARTIN. Then say what you mean.

HANS. All right, if that's what you want, I'll say just what I
mean. I think a man murders himself in these places.

MARTIN [*crossing* U C *and* R]. I kill no one but myself.

HANS. I don't care. I tell you it gives me the creeps. And that's why I couldn't bring your mother, if you want to know.

MARTIN [*crossing* D R]. The Gospels are the only mother I've ever had.

HANS [*triumphantly, rising*]. And haven't you ever read in the Gospels, don't you know what's written in there? "Thou shalt honor thy father and thy mother."

MARTIN. You're not understanding me, because you don't want to.

HANS [*crossing up and* R, *reaching* MARTIN *at end of speech*]. That's fine talk, oh, yes, fine, holy talk, but it won't wash, Martin. It won't wash because you can't ever, however you try, you can't get away from your body because that's what you live in, and it's all you've got to die in, and you can't get away from the body of your father and your mother! We're bodies, Martin, and we're bound together for always. But you're like every man who was ever born into this world, Martin. You'd like to pretend that it was *you* who made you—and not the body of a woman and another man.

MARTIN [*evading* HANS, *crossing* C *and* U L]. Churches, kings and fathers—why do they ask so much, and why do they all of them get so much more than they deserve?

HANS. You think so. Well, I think I deserve a little more than you've given me.

MARTIN [*whirling back to* C]. I've given you! I don't have to give you! I *am*—that's all I need to give to you. That's your big reward, and that's all you're ever going to get, and it's more than any father's got a right to. You wanted me to learn Latin, to be a Master of Arts, be a lawyer. All you want is me to justify *you!* Well, I can't, and, what's more, I won't. I can't even justify myself. So just stop asking me what have I accomplished, and what have I done for you. I've done all for you I'll ever do, and that's live and wait to die.

HANS. Why do you blame *me* for everything?

MARTIN [*crossing* D C, *sitting on right end of downstage bench*]. I don't blame you. I'm just not grateful, that's all.

HANS [*crossing* C *to* MARTIN]. Listen, I'm not a specially good man, I know, but I believe in God and in Jesus Christ His Son, perhaps, and I can make some sort of life for myself that has a little joy in it somewhere. But where is your joy? You wrote to me once, when you were at the University, that only Christ could light up the place you live in, but what's the point? if it turns out the place you're living in is just a hovel? Don't you think it mightn't be better not to see at all?

MARTIN. I'd rather be able to see.

HANS. You'd rather see! [*Crosses* U L *above table.*]

MARTIN. You really are disappointed, aren't you?

HANS [*crossing* D L *around table*]. And why? I see a young man, learned and full of life, my son, abusing his youth with fear and humiliation. You think you're facing up to it in here, but you're not; you're running away.

MARTIN. If it's so easy in here, why do you think the rest of the world isn't knocking the gates down to get in?

HANS [*in front of table*]. Because they haven't given up, that's why.

MARTIN. Well, there it is; you think I've given up.

HANS. Yes, there it is. [*Sits at left end of downstage bench.*] That damned monk's wine has given me a headache.

MARTIN. I'm sorry.

HANS. Yes, we're all sorry, and a lot of good it does any of us.

MARTIN. I suppose fathers and sons always disappoint each other.

HANS. I worked for you, I went without for you.

MARTIN. Well?

HANS. Well! [*Almost anxiously.*] And if I beat you fairly often and pretty hard sometimes, I suppose it wasn't any more than any other boy, was it?

MARTIN. No.

HANS. What do you think it is makes you different? Other

men are all right, aren't they? You were stubborn, you were always stubborn, you've always had to resist, haven't you?

MARTIN. You disappointed me, too, and not just a few times, but at some time of every day I ever remember hearing or seeing you, but, as you say, maybe that was also no more than any other boy. But I loved you the best. Funnily enough, my mother disappointed me the most, and I loved her less, much less. It was always *you* I wanted. And if anyone was to hold me, I wanted it to be you. She beat me once for stealing a nut, your wife. I remember it so well, she beat me until the blood came; I was so surprised to see it on my fingertips. Yes, stealing a nut, that's right. On that day, for the first time, the pain belonged to me and no one else, it went no further than *my* body, bent between *my* knees and *my* chin. But that's not the point. I had corns on my backside already. But always before, when you beat me for something, the pain seemed outside of me in some way, as if it belonged to the rest of the world, and not only me.

HANS. I don't know what any of that means; I really don't. You know what, Martin, I think you've always been scared —ever since you could get up off your knees and walk. Like that day, that day when you were coming home from Erfurt, and the thunderstorm broke, and you were so scared, you lay on the ground and cried out to St. Anne because you saw a bit of lightning and thought you'd seen a vision.

MARTIN. I saw it all right!

HANS. . . . and you went and asked her to save you—on condition that you became a monk.

MARTIN. I saw it.

HANS. Did you? [*Rises and crosses* R *above table.*] So it's still St. Anne, is it? I thought you were blaming your mother and me for your damned monkery!

MARTIN. Perhaps I should.

HANS [*crossing* D C *to* MARTIN]. And perhaps you should have another little think about that heavenly vision that wangled you away into the cloister.

MARTIN. What do you mean?

HANS. I mean: I hope it really was a vision. I hope it wasn't a delusion and some trick of the devil's. I really hope so, because I couldn't bear to think of it otherwise. [*Breaks away, crosses above table, picks up hat from bench.*] Good-by, son. I'm sorry we had to quarrel. It shouldn't have turned out like this at all today. [*Pause.*]

MARTIN. Father—why did you give your consent?

HANS. What, to the monkery, you mean?

MARTIN. Yes. You could have refused, but why didn't you?

HANS. Well, when your two brothers died with the plague . . .

MARTIN. You gave me up for dead, didn't you?

HANS [*crossing D L, then picking up mug from table*]. Good-by, son. Here—have a drink of holy wine. [*He goes out.* MARTIN *sits with the mug in his hand and looks into it. Then he drinks from it slowly, as if for the first time. Then he looks up, agonized.*]

MARTIN. But what if it isn't true?

CURTAIN

DECOR NOTE: After the intense private interior of Act I, with its outer darkness and simple objects, the physical effect from now on should be more intricate, general, less personal, sweeping, concerned with men in time rather than particular man in the unconscious; caricature, not portraiture, like the popular woodcuts of the period, like Dürer.

ACT TWO

Scene One

AT RISE OF CURTAIN: *The stage is clear but for the towering walls. The crucifix is gone. The* KNIGHT *stands* C *in bright sunlight.*

KNIGHT. The Market Place, Jütebog, ten years later!

[*The* KNIGHT *exits* U R. *There is a thump of drums, and a raucous and rousing rendition of the* Ave Vera *commences from off* U L *followed by the immediate entrance of the Tetzel procession. Two smudged and tousled children in cassocks lead with finger cymbals, followed by monks with tambourines, drums, cymbals, a banner with the Pope's arms insignia, and two monks dragging a cart which is bedecked with fringe and tassels. In the cart stands* TETZEL, *the focus of the procession, Dominican, inquisitor, and the most famed and successful indulgence vendor of his day. He is splendidly equipped to be an ecclesiastical huckster, with alive, silver hair, the powerfully calculating voice, range and technique of a trained orator, the terrible riveting charm of a dedicated professional able to winkle coppers out of the pockets of the poor and desperate. He is holding a large red cross, and behind him hangs a painting of the Madonna with hovering angels. The procession moves to* C, *then straight downstage, and divides* R *and* L. *The cart is drawn to* C, *leaving the monks arranged on either side. The cart pullers drop the tongue and while one steadies the cart the other lifts down a set of steps which he hooks over the side of the cart and then stands at the right of the steps to receive the red cross from Tetzel. The monks are in white Dominican habits with black capes. They are ruddy from outdoor life and a bit the worse for wear. They are a tough-looking group, capable of fending off bandits and acting as*

*Tetzel's bodyguards as he travels the countryside touting
indulgences. They have obviously heard Tetzel's spiel many
times and are generally relaxed, but they nevertheless support
him with vigor at certain points in his diatribe. The song
ends with a crash of cymbals.* TETZEL *surveys the audience
fiercely, and begins.*]

TETZEL. Are you wondering who I am, or what I am? Is there
anyone here among you, any small child, any cripple, or any
sick idiot who hasn't heard of me, and doesn't know why I
am here? No? No? Well, speak up then if there is? What,
no one? Do you all know me, then? Do you all know who
I am? [TETZEL *hands cross down and leaves cart for* D C.]
If it's true, it's very good, and just as it should be. Just as
it should be, and no more than that! However—just in case,
mind, there is one blind, maimed midget among you today
who can't hear, I will open his ears and wash them out
with sacred soap! And as for the rest of you, I know I can
rely on you all to listen patiently while I instruct him. Is
that right? Can I go on? I'm asking you, is that right, can
I go on? I say, "can I go on"?
[*Pause. Hopeful that a member of the audience will say
"Yes."*]
Thank you. And what is there to tell this blind, maimed
midget down there somewhere among you? No, don't look
'round for him, you'll only scare him and then he'll lose his
one great chance, and it's not likely to come again, or if it
does come, maybe it'll be too late. Well, what's the good
news on this bright day? What's the information you want?
It's this! Who is this friar with his red cross? Who sent
him, and what's he here for? No! Don't try to work it out
for yourself because I'm going to tell you now, this very
minute. I am John Tetzel, Dominican, inquisitor, sub-com-
missioner to the Archbishop of Mainz, and what I bring
you is indulgences. Indulgences made possible by the red
blood of Jesus Christ, and the red cross you see standing
up here behind me is the standard of those who carry them.
[MONK *with cross moves down and across stage, taking po-*

sition at Tetzel's left.] Look at it! Take a good look at it!
What else do you see up there? Well, what do they look
like? [MONK *with arms steps forward, then back into place.*]
Why, it's the arms of his holiness, because why? Because
it's him who sent me here. Yes, my friend, the Pope himself
has sent me with indulgences for you! Fine, you say, but
what are indulgences? And what are they to me? What are
indulgences? They're only the most precious and noble of
God's gifts to men, that's all they are! Before God, I tell
you I wouldn't swap my privilege at this moment with that
of St. Peter in Heaven because I've already saved more souls
with my indulgences than he could ever have done with all
his sermons. You think that's bragging, do you? Well, listen
a little more carefully, my friend, because this concerns *you!*
Just look at it this way. For every mortal sin you commit,
the Church says that after confession and contrition, you've
got to do penance—either in this life or in purgatory—for
seven years. Seven years! Right? Are you with me? Good.
Now then, how many mortal sins are committed by you—
by you—in a single day? Just think for one moment: in
one single day of your life. Can you find the answer? Oh,
not so much as one a day. Very well then, how many in a
month? How many in six months? How many in a year?
And how many in a whole lifetime? Yes, you needn't fidget
in your seat—it doesn't bear thinking about, does it? Try
and add up all the years of torment piling up!

[*Cymbal crash. Drum thumps out three beats. One* MONK
*moves above cart for indulgence pole, hung back of the
Madonna painting, and waits for entrance.*] What about
it? And isn't there anything you can do about this terrible situation you're in? Do you really want to know?
Yes! There is something, and that something I have here
with me today: letters, letters of indulgence. [*Accompanied by a drum roll, the* MONK *brings the indulgence pole
from behind the cart with a flourish.*] Hold up the letters so
that everyone can see them. Look at them, all properly
sealed, an indulgence in every envelope, and one of them

can be yours today, now, before it's too late! Look at them!
Take a good look! [MONK *crosses in front of* TETZEL, *showing indulgences, and takes position at left of monk with
cross.*] There isn't any one sin so big that one of these letters
can't remit it. I challenge any one here, any member of this
audience, to present me with a sin, anything, any kind of a
sin, I don't care what it is, that I can't settle for him with
one of these precious little envelopes. Why, if anyone had
ever offered violence to the blessed Virgin Mary, Mother of
God, if he'd only pay up—as long as he paid up all he could
—he'd find himself forgiven. You think I'm exaggerating?
You do, do you? Well, I'm authorized to go even further
than that. Not only am I empowered to give you these letters
of pardon for the sins you've already committed, I can pardon you for those sins you haven't even committed.
[*Pause . . . then slowly.*]
But, which, however, you *intend* to commit! But, you ask—
and it's a fair question—why is our Holy Lord prepared to
distribute such a rich grace to me? The answer, my friends,
is all too simple. It's so that we can restore the ruined
church of St. Peter and St. Paul in Rome! So that it won't
have its equal anywhere in the world. This great church
contains the bodies not only of the holy apostles Peter and
Paul, but of a hundred thousand martyrs and no less than
forty-six popes! To say nothing of the relics like St. Veron-
ica's handkerchief, the burning bush of Moses and the very
rope with which Judas Iscariot hanged himself! But, alas,
my friends, this fine old building is threatened with destruc-
tion, and all these things with it, unless a sufficient restora-
tion fund is raised, and raised soon. [*With passionate irony.*]
. . . Will anyone dare to say that the cause is not a good
one?
[*Pause. Cymbal crash, drum thumps four times. The children move to the cart and take down a chest which they
place before* TETZEL, *opened.*]
. . . So won't you, for as little as one quarter of a florin, my
friend, buy yourself one of these letters, so that in the hour

of death, the gate of paradise be flung open for you? And, these letters aren't just for the living but for the dead, too. There can't be one amongst you who hasn't at least one dear one who has departed—and to *who knows what?* [*Three small, ominous drum beats, echoing Tetzel's tempo.*] So don't hold back, come forward, think of your dear ones, think of yourselves! For twelve groats, or whatever it is we think you can afford, you can rescue your father from agony and yourself from certain disaster. And if you only have the coat on your back, then strip it off, strip it off now so that you can obtain grace. For remember: As soon as your money rattles in the box and the cash bell rings, the soul flies out of purgatory and sings! So, come on, then. Get your money out! [*Tambourines shake and drums roll, ending with cymbal crash.* TETZEL *stares unbelieving at empty box, then resumes on a grim note.*] What is it, have your wits flown away with your faith? Listen, soon, I shall take down the cross, shut the gates of heaven, and put out the brightness of this sun of grace that shines on you here today. The Lord our God reigns no longer. He has resigned all power to the Pope.
[TETZEL *takes the red cross from the monk, holds it out over the audience and blesses them with it as the group moves in, rolling drums and shaking tambourines as the lights start to fade.*]
In the name of the Father, and of the Son and of the Holy Ghost. Amen. In the name of the Father, and of the Son and of the Holy Ghost. Amen. In the name of the Father, and of the Son and of the Holy Ghost. Amen.
[*When it is dark, there is a cymbal crash beginning the* Ave Vera *which is sung, fading into the distance, as the stage is cleared.*]

BLACKOUT

ACT TWO

Scene Two

SCENE: *The* Ave Vera *fades in the distance and a solo voice is heard singing the* Salve Regina. *The lights come up in a sunny, leafy pattern. The stage is clear but for one chair placed* D L. *Over it hangs a gnarled tree branch. The* KNIGHT *is discovered standing just back of the chair.*]

KNIGHT. The Garden of the Eremite Cloister, Wittenberg, fifteen hundred and seventeen.

[*The* KNIGHT *moves briskly to center stage as the lights build. He turns to watch* STAUPITZ *entering* D L, *wearing spectacles, reading a breviary.*]

KNIGHT. Johan von Staupitz, Vicar General of the Augustinian Order. [*The* KNIGHT *exits smartly* U L.]

[STAUPITZ *is a quiet, gentle-voiced man in late middle age, almost stolidly contemplative. He has profound respect for Martin, recognizing in him the powerful potential of insight, sensitivity, courage and also heroics that is quite outside the range of his own endeavor. However, he also understands that a man of his own limitations can offer a great deal to such a young man at this point in his development, and his treatment of Martin is a successfully astringent mixture of sympathy and ridicule. Birds sing as he sits in his chair to read.* MARTIN *approaches from* U R *and there is a flurry of bird-sound. They are silent for a while and then are heard intermittently throughout the scene.*]

MARTIN [*prostrating himself before* STAUPITZ, *who blesses him; looking up*]. The birds always seem to fly away the moment I come out here.

STAUPITZ. Birds, unfortunately, have no faith.

MARTIN [*sitting on ground* C]. Perhaps it's simply that they don't like me.

STAUPITZ [*pointedly*]. They haven't learned yet that you mean them no harm, that's all.

MARTIN [*wary*]. Are you treating me to one of your allegories?

STAUPITZ. Well, you recognized it, anyway.

MARTIN. I ought to. Ever since I came into the cloister, I've become a craftsman allegory maker myself. Only last week I was lecturing on Galatians Three, verse three, and I allegorized going to the lavatory.

STAUPITZ [*quoting the verse*]. "Are ye so foolish that what ye have begun in the spirit, ye would now end in the flesh."

MARTIN. That's right. But allegories aren't much help in theology except to decorate a house that's been already built by argument.

STAUPITZ. Well, it's a house you've been able to unlock for a great many of us. I never dreamed when I first came here to Wittenberg that the University's reputation would ever become what it has, and in such a short time, and it's mostly due to you.

MARTIN [*very deliberately turning the compliment*]. If ever a man could get to Heaven through monkery, that man would be me.

STAUPITZ. You know quite well what I mean. I'm talking about your scholarship, and what you manage to do with it, not your monkery, as you call it. The only wonder is that you haven't killed yourself with your prayers, and watchings —yes, and even your reading, too. All these trials and tribulations you go through, they're meat and drink to you.

MARTIN [*patient*]. Will you ever stop lecturing me about this?

STAUPITZ. Of course not. Why do you think you come here— to see me in the garden when you could be inside working?

MARTIN. Well, if it'll please you, I've so little time, what with my lectures and study, I'm scarcely able to carry out even the basic requirements of the Rule.

STAUPITZ. I'm delighted to hear it. You've always been obsessed with the Rule because it serves very nicely as a protection for you.

MARTIN. What protection?

STAUPITZ. Brother Martin, don't pretend to look so innocent. Protection against the demands of your own instincts, that's what. You see, you think you admire authority, and so you do, but unfortunately, you can't submit to it. So, what you do, by your exaggerated attention to the Rule, is to make that authority ridiculous. And the reason you do that is because you're determined to substitute for that authority something else—yourself.

MARTIN. Myself?

STAUPITZ [*rising, crossing* D L *and up, to lean on back of chair*]. Oh, come along, Martin, I've been Vicar General too long not to have made that little discovery. Anyway, you shouldn't be too concerned with a failing like that. It also provides the strongest kind of security.

MARTIN. Security? I don't feel *that*.

STAUPITZ. I dare say, but you've got it all the same, which is more than most of us have.

MARTIN. And how have I managed to come by this strange security?

STAUPITZ. Quite simply: by demanding of yourself an impossible standard of perfection.

MARTIN. I don't see what work or merit can come from a heart like mine.

STAUPITZ. Oh, my dear, dear friend, I've sworn a thousand times to Almighty God to live piously, and have I been able to keep my vows? No, of course I haven't. If God won't be merciful to me for the love of Christ when I leave this world, I shan't stand before Him on account of all my vows and good works, I shall perish, that's all.

MARTIN. You think I lavish too much attention on my own pain, don't you?

STAUPITZ. Well, that's difficult for me to say, Martin. We're very different kinds of men, you and I. Yes, you do lavish attention on yourself, but then a large man is worth the pains he takes. Like St. Paul, some men must say, "I die daily."

MARTIN [*rising impatiently, crossing* R]. Father, have you never felt humiliated to feel that you belong to a world that's dying?

STAUPITZ. No, I don't think I have.

MARTIN. Surely, this must be the last age of time we're living in. There can't be any more left but the black bottom of the bucket.

STAUPITZ. Do you mean the Last Judgment?

MARTIN. No, I don't mean that. The Last Judgment isn't to come. It's here and now.

STAUPITZ. Good. That's a little better, anyway.

MARTIN. I'm like a ripe stool in the world's straining anus, and at any moment we're about to let each other go.

STAUPITZ [*crossing to* MARTIN]. There's nothing new in the world being damned, dying or without hope. It's always been like that, and it'll stay like it. What's the matter with you? What are you making faces for?

MARTIN. It's nothing, Father, just a—a slight discomfort.

STAUPITZ. Slight discomfort? There's always something the matter with you, Brother Martin. If it's not the gripes, insomnia, or faith and works, it's boils or indigestion or some kind of bellyache you've got. All these severe fasts——

MARTIN. That's what my father says.

STAUPITZ. Your father sounds pretty sensible to me.

MARTIN. He is, and you know, he's a theologian, too. He always knew that works alone don't save any man. Mind you, he never said anything about faith coming first.

STAUPITZ [*turning away to move* L]. You see, your father's taken a vow of poverty too, even though it's very different from your own. And he took it the day he told himself, and told *you,* that he was a complete man, or at least, *a contented man.*

MARTIN [*with increasing exasperation*]. A pig waffling in its own crap is contented.

STAUPITZ. Exactly.

MARTIN. My father, faced with an unfamiliar notion, is like a cow staring at a new barn door. Like those who look on the cross and see nothing.

STAUPITZ [*turning back and laughing*]. One thing I promise you, Martin. You'll never be a spectator. You'll always take part.

MARTIN [*has to smile at himself*]. How is it somehow you always manage to comfort me?

STAUPITZ. Sometimes modest sponges are best at quenching big thirsts. How's your tummy?

MARTIN. Better.

STAUPITZ [*smiling, too*]. Did you know the Duke's been complaining to me about you? [*Puts arm across* MARTIN'S *shoulders, walks him* R.]

MARTIN [*stopping*]. Why, what have I done?

STAUPITZ. Preaching against indulgences again.

MARTIN [*starting* R *again*]. Oh, that—I was very mild.

STAUPITZ [*following*]. Yes, well, I've heard your mildness in the pulpit. When I think of the terror it used to be for you —you used to fall up the steps with fright. Sheer fright! You were too frightened to become a Doctor of Theology, and you wouldn't be now if I hadn't forced you. "I'm too weak, I shan't live long enough!" Do you remember what I said to you?

MARTIN. "Never mind, the Lord still has work to do in Heaven, and there are always vacancies."

STAUPITZ. Remember, the Duke paid all the expenses of your promotion for you. He was very cross when he spoke to me. He said you even made some reference to the collection of holy relics in the Castle Church, and most of those were paid for by the sale of indulgences, as you know. Did you say anything about them?

MARTIN. Well, yes, but not about those in the Castle Church. I did make some point in passing about someone who claimed to have a feather from the wing of the angel Gabriel.

STAUPITZ [*crossing to* C]. Oh, yes, I heard about that.

MARTIN. And I just finished off by saying how is it that Christ had twelve apostles, and eighteen of them are buried in Germany.

STAUPITZ [*crossing* L]. Well, the Duke's coming to hear your next sermon for himself, so try to keep off the subject. It's All Saints' Day soon, remember, and all those relics will be out on show for everyone to gawk at. The Duke's a good chap, and he's very proud of his collection, and it doesn't help to be rude about it.

MARTIN. I've tried to keep off the subject because I haven't been by any means sure about it. Then I did make a few mild protests in a couple of sermons.

STAUPITZ. Yes, yes, but what did you actually say?

MARTIN. That you can't strike bargains with God. Am I right?

STAUPITZ [*crossing to chair and sitting*]. Yes, what's difficult to understand is why your sermons are so popular.

MARTIN [*following*]. Well, there are plenty who sit out there stiff with hatred. It's about all this. The other day a man was brought to me, a shoemaker. His wife had just died, and I said to him, "What've you done for her?" so he said, "I've buried her and commended her soul to God." "But haven't you had a Mass said for the repose of her soul?" "No," he said, "what's the point? She entered Heaven the moment she died." "How do you know that?" And he said, "Well, I've got proof, that's why." And out of his pocket he took a letter of indulgence.

STAUPITZ. Ah.

MARTIN. He threw it at me, and said, "And if you still maintain that a Mass is necessary, then my wife's been swindled by our most holy father the Pope. Or, if not by him, then by the priest who sold it to me."

STAUPITZ. Tetzel.

MARTIN. Who else?

STAUPITZ. That old tout!

MARTIN. There's another story going around about him which is obviously true, because I've checked it at several sources. It seems that a certain Saxon nobleman heard Tetzel in Jüte-

bog. After he had finished his usual performance, he asked
him if he'd repeat what he'd said at one stage, about having
the power of pardoning sins men intend to commit. Tetzel
was very high and mighty, you know what he's like, and
said, "Of course, weren't you listening? Of course I can
give pardon not only for sins already committed but for sins
that men *intend* to commit." "Well, then, that's fine," says
this nobleman, "because I'd like to take revenge on one of
my enemies. Nothing much, I don't want to kill him or
anything like that. Just a little slight revenge. Now, if I
give you ten guilden, will you give me a letter of indulgence
that will justify me—justify me freely and completely?"
Well, it seems Tetzel made a few stock objections, but eventually agreed on thirty guilden; they made a deal. The man
went on his way with his letter of indulgence, and Tetzel
set out for his next job, which was Leipzig. Well, half way
between Leipzig and Treblen, in the middle of a wood, he
was set on by a band of thugs, and beaten up. While he's
lying there on the grass in a pool of his own blood, he looks
up and sees that one of them is the Saxon nobleman and
that they're making off with his great trunk full of money.
The moment he's recovered enough, he rushes back to Jütebog, takes the nobleman to court. What does the nobleman
do? Takes out the letter of indulgence, shows it to Duke
George—case dismissed!

STAUPITZ [*laughing*]. Well, I leave you to handle it. But try
and be careful. Remember, *I* agree with everything you say,
but the moment someone disagrees or objects to what you're
saying, *that* will be the moment when you'll suddenly rec-
ognize the strength of your belief!

MARTIN. Father, I'm never sure of the words till I hear them
out loud.

STAUPITZ [*rising, crossing to* MARTIN *a bit*]. Well, perhaps
that's the meaning of the Word. The Word is me, and I
am the Word. Anyway, try and be a little prudent. Look at
Erasmus: He never really gets into any serious trouble, but
he still manages to make his point.

MARTIN. People like Erasmus get upset because I talk of pigs and Christ in the same breath.

STAUPITZ. Well, you might be right. Erasmus is a fine scholar, but there are too many scholars who think they're better simply because they insinuate in Latin what you'll say in plain German. Don't forget—you began this affair in the name of Our Lord Jesus Christ. You must do as God commands you, of course, but remember, St. Jerome once wrote about a philosopher who destroyed his own eyes so that it would give him more freedom to study. Take care of your eyes, my son, and do something about those damned bowels! [*Crosses* D R.]

MARTIN [*crossing* U L]. I will. Who knows? If I break wind in Wittenberg, they might smell me in Rome. [*Exit* U L. *Organ music, harsh and somber, fills the air.*]

BLACKOUT

ACT TWO

Scene Three

SCENE: *The* KNIGHT *is discovered in his shaft of light* D L. *The organ fades down as he announces:*]

KNIGHT. The Castle Church, Wittenberg, the Eve of All Saints.

[*The* KNIGHT *exits* D L *as the lights build. There is a pulpit at center stage. It is paneled with dark wood, and a stair twists up the left side.* MARTIN *enters from* U R, *carrying a Bible and a white prayer stole. He crosses to the* D L *light, genuflects, kisses the stole and places it over his shoulders as he ascends the pulpit. He places the Bible before him, opens it to a marked place.*]

MARTIN. My text is from the Epistle of Paul the Apostle to the Romans, chapter one, verse seventeen: "For therein is the righteousness of God revealed from faith to faith."
[*Pause.*]

We are living in a dangerous time. You may not think so, but it could be that this is the most dangerous time since the light first broke upon the earth. It may not be true, but it's very probably true—but, what's most important is that it's an assumption we are obliged to make. We Christians seem to be wise outwardly and mad inwardly, and in this Jerusalem we have built there are blasphemies flourishing that make the Jews no worse than giggling children. A man is not a good Christian because he understands Greek and Hebrew. Jerome knew five languages, but he's inferior to Augustine, who knew only one. Of course, Erasmus wouldn't agree with me, but perhaps one day the Lord will open his eyes for him. But listen! A man without Christ becomes his own shell. We are content to be shells. Shells filled with small trinkets. And, what are the trinkets? Today is the eve of All Saints, and the holy relics will be on show to you all; to the hungry ones whose lives are made satisfied by trinkets, by an imposing procession and the dressings up of all kinds of dismal things. You'll mumble for magic with lighted candles to St. Anthony for your erysipelas; to St. Valentine for your epilepsy; to St. Appolonia if you've got the toothache, and to St. Louis to stop your beer from going sour. And tomorrow you'll queue for hours outside the Castle Church so that you can get a cheap-rate glimpse of St. Jerome's tooth, or four pieces each of St. Chrysostom and St. Augustine, and six of St. Bernard. The deacons will have to link hands to hold you back while you struggle to gawk at four hairs from Our Lady's head, at the pieces of her girdle and her veil stained with her Son's blood. You'll sleep outside in the streets with the garbage all night so that you can stuff your eyes like roasting birds on a scrap of swaddling clothes, eleven pieces from the original crib, one wisp of straw from the manger, and a gold coin specially minted by three wise men for the occasion. Your emptiness will be frothing over at the sight of a strand of Jesus' beard, at one of the nails driven into His hands, and at the remains of the loaf from the Last Supper. Shells for shells, empty things for empty men. There are some who complain of these things, but they write in Latin for scholars. Who'll speak out in rough German? Someone's got to bell the cat! For you must be made to know that there's no security, there's no security at all, either in indulgences, holy busy-work or anywhere in this world. It came to me while I was in my tower, what they call the monk's sweathouse, the jakes, the john or whatever you're pleased to call it. I was struggling with the text I've given you: "For therein is the righteousness of God revealed, from faith to faith; as it is written, the just shall live by faith." And seated there, on that privy, my head down, just as when I was a little boy, I couldn't reach down to my breath for the sickness in my bowels, and I seemed to sense beneath me a large rat, a heavy, wet, plague rat, slashing at my privates with its death's teeth.

I thought of the righteousness of God, and wished His gospel had never been put to paper for men to read; who demanded my love and made it impossible to return it. And I sat in my heap of pain until the words emerged and opened out. "The just shall live by faith." My pain vanished, my bowels flushed and I could get up. I could see the life I'd lost. No man is just because he does just works. The works are just if the man is just. If a man doesn't believe in Christ, not only are his sins mortal, but his good works. This I know: Reason is the devil's whore, born of one stinking goat called Aristotle, which believes that good works make a good man. But the truth is that the just shall live by faith alone. I need no more than my sweet Redeemer and Mediator, Jesus Christ, and I shall go on praising Him as long as I have voice to sing; and if anyone doesn't care to sing with me, then he can howl on his own. If we are going to be deserted, let's follow the deserted Christ. [*Choir sings Laudes Christo,* MARTIN *blesses the congregation, then murmurs a prayer, and descends from the pulpit, as lights fade.*]

ACT TWO
Scene Four

SCENE: *The* KNIGHT *is discovered in his shaft of light* D L. *The choir fades as he announces:*]

KNIGHT. The Fugger Palace, Augsburg, fifteen hundred and eighteen.

[*The lights build, revealing a paneled wall stage* R. *Through an opening is seen a painting of the crucifixion in muted tones. There is one ornately carved chair and a small table on which lie two tied scrolls, set just before this archway.* CAJETAN *appears from* R *and stops in front of the set as the* KNIGHT *announces:*]

KNIGHT. Thomas de Vio, known as Cajetan, Cardinal of San Sisto, General of the Dominican Order.

[*The* KNIGHT *exits* U L. CAJETAN, *dressed in a voluminous red cloak and helmet-like cap, is a distinguished theologian, Papal legate, and Rome's highest representative in Germany. He is about fifty but youthful, with a shrewd, broad outlook, quite the opposite of the vulgar bigotry of* TETZEL, *who enters* D L.]

TETZEL. He's here.
CAJETAN. So I see.
TETZEL. What do you mean?
CAJETAN. You look so cross. Is Staupitz with him?

TETZEL. Yes. At least *he's* polite.

CAJETAN [*crossing to* TETZEL]. I know Staupitz. From all accounts, he has a deep regard for this monk—which is all to the good from our point of view.

TETZEL. He's worried, you can see that. These Augustinians, they don't have much fibre.

CAJETAN. What about Dr. Luther? What's he got to say for himself?

TETZEL. Too much. I said to him if our Lord the Pope were to offer you a good bishopric and a plenary indulgence for repairing your church, you'd soon start singing a different song.

CAJETAN. Dear, oh, dear, and what did he say to that?

TETZEL. He asked me——

CAJETAN. Well?

TETZEL. He asked me how was my mother's syphilis.

CAJETAN. It's a fair question in the circumstances. You Germans, you're a crude lot.

TETZEL. That's what I said to him—— "These Italians, they're different. They're not just learned, they're subtle, experienced antagonists. You'll get slung in the fire after five minutes."

CAJETAN. And?

TETZEL. He said, "I've only been to Italy once, and they didn't look very subtle to me. They were lifting their legs on street corners like dogs."

CAJETAN. I hope he didn't see any cardinals at it. Knowing some of them, it's not impossible. Well, let's have a look at this foul-mouthed monk of yours.

TETZEL. Very well, your eminence. I hope he behaves properly. I've spoken to him.

[TETZEL *goes out.* CAJETAN *crosses to chair and sits as* TETZEL *returns with* MARTIN, *who advances, prostrates himself, his face to the ground before Cajetan.* CAJETAN *blesses him and* MARTIN *rises to a kneeling position where* CAJETAN *studies him.* TETZEL *stands* D R.]

CAJETAN [*courteous*]. Please stand up, Dr. Luther. [MARTIN *rises.*] So you're the one they call the excessive doctor. You don't look excessive to me. Do you feel very excessive?

MARTIN [*conscious of being patronized*]. It's one of those words which can be used like a harness on a man.

CAJETAN. How do you mean?

MARTIN. I mean it has very little meaning beyond traducing him.

CAJETAN. Quite. There's never been any doubt in my mind that you've been misinterpreted all 'round, and, as you say, traduced. Well, what a surprise you are! Here was I expecting to see some doddering old theologian with dust in his ears who could be bullied into a heart attack by Tetzel here in half an hour. And here you are, as gay and sprightly as a young bull. How old are you, my son?

MARTIN. Thirty-four, most worthy father.

CAJETAN. Tetzel, he's a boy—you didn't tell me! And how long have you been wearing your doctor's ring?

MARTIN. Five years——

CAJETAN. So you were only twenty-nine! Well, obviously, everything I've heard about you is true—you must be a very remarkable young man. I wouldn't have believed there was one doctor in the whole of Germany under fifty. Would you, Brother John?

TETZEL. I certainly wouldn't.

CAJETAN. What is surprising, frankly, is that they allowed such an honor to be conferred on anyone so young and inexperienced as a man must inevitably be at twenty-nine. [*He smiles to let his point get home.*] Your father must be a proud man.

MARTIN [*irritated*]. Not at all. I should say he was disappointed and constantly apprehensive.

CAJETAN. Really? Well, that's surely one of the legacies of parenthood to offset the incidental pleasures. [TETZEL *crosses to stand at Cajetan's right, prepared to handle scrolls.*] Now then, to business. I was saying to Tetzel, I don't think this matter need take up very much of our time. But, before we do start, there's just one thing I would like to say, and that is I was sorry you should have decided to ask the Emperor for safe conduct. That was hardly necessary, my son, and it's a little—well, distressing to feel you have such an opinion of us, such a lack of trust in your mother church, and in those who have, I can assure you, your dearest interests at heart.

MARTIN [*outmaneuvered*]. I—only thought that considering the present situation . . .

CAJETAN [*kindly*]. But never mind all that now, that's behind us, and, in the long run, it's unimportant, after all, isn't it? Your Vicar General has come with you, hasn't he?

MARTIN. He's outside.

CAJETAN. I've known Staupitz for years. You have a wonderful friend there.

MARTIN. I know. I—have great love for him.

CAJETAN. And he has for you, too, I know. Oh, my dear, dear son, this is such a ridiculous, unnecessary business for us all to be mixed up in. It's such a tedious, upsetting affair, and what purpose is there in it? Your entire order in Germany has been brought into disgrace. I have my job to do, and, make no mistake, it isn't all honey for an Italian legate in your country. You know how it is, people are inclined to resent you. Nationalist feeling and all that—which I respect —but it does complicate one's task to the point where this kind of issue thrown in for good measure simply makes the whole operation impossible. You know what I mean? [*Rises, crosses* L.] I mean, there's your Duke Frederick, an absolutely fair, honest man, if ever there was one, and one his holiness values and esteems particularly. Well, his holiness instructed me to present the Duke with the Golden Rose of Virtue, so you can see. As well as even more indulgences for his Castle Church. But what happens now? Because of all this unpleasantness and the uproar it's caused throughout Germany, the Duke's put in an extremely difficult position about accepting it. Naturally, he wants to do the right thing by everyone. But he's not going to betray you or anything like that, however much he's set his heart on that Golden Rose, all these years. And, of course he's perfectly right. I know he has the greatest regard for you and for some of your ideas—even though, as he's told me—he doesn't agree with a lot of them. No, I can only respect him for all that. [*Returning to chair and sitting.*] So, you see, my dear son, what a mess we are in. Now, what are we going to do? Um? The Duke is unhappy. I am unhappy, his holiness is unhappy, and, you, my son, you are unhappy.

MARTIN [*formal, as if it were a prepared speech*]. Most worthy father, in obedience to the summons of his papal holiness, and in obedience to the orders of my gracious lord, the Elector of Saxony, I have come before you as a submissive and dutiful son of the holy Catholic church, and if I have been wrong, to submit to your instruction in the truth.

CAJETAN [*impatiently*]. My son, you have upset all Germany with your dispute about indulgences. I know you're a very learned doctor of the Holy Scriptures, and that you've already aroused a few supporters. But if you wish to remain a member of the Church, and to find a gracious father in the Pope, you'd better listen. [*Holds out hand, in which* TETZEL *places scroll.*] I have here, in front of me, three propositions which, by the command of our holy father, Pope Leo the Tenth, I shall put to you now. First, you must admit your faults, and retract all your errors and sermons. Secondly, you must promise to abstain from propagating your opinions at any time in the future. And, thirdly, you must behave generally with greater moderation, and avoid anything which might cause offense or grieve and disturb the Church.

MARTIN. May I be allowed to see the Pope's instruction?

CAJETAN. No, my dear son, you may not. [*Handing scroll back to* TETZEL.] All you are required to do is confess your errors, keep a strict watch on your words, and not go back like a dog to his vomit. Then, once you have done that, I have been authorized by our most holy father to put everything to rights again.

MARTIN. I understand all that. But I'm asking you to tell me where I have erred.

CAJETAN. If you insist. [*Stands, taking second scroll from* TETZEL *and crossing* L, *rattling off, very fast.*] Just to begin with, here are two propositions you have advanced, and which you will have to retract before anything else. First, the treasure of indulgences does not consist of the sufferings and torments of our Lord Jesus Christ. Second, the man who receives the holy sacrament must have faith in the grace that is presented to him. [*Turns back.*] Enough?

MARTIN [*facing* L *to* CAJETAN]. I rest my case entirely on Holy Scriptures.

CAJETAN. The Pope alone has power and authority over all those things.

MARTIN. Except Scripture.

CAJETAN. Including Scripture. What do you mean?

MARTIN. I mean that . . .

TETZEL [*crossing to* MARTIN]. Only the Pope has the right to interpret the meaning of Scripture. The Pope's judgment cannot err, whether it concerns the Christian faith or anything that has to do with the salvation of the human race.

MARTIN. That sounds like your theses.

TETZEL. Burned in the market place by your students in Wittenberg—thank you very much.

MARTIN. I assure you, I had nothing to do with that.

CAJETAN. Of course. Brother John wasn't suggesting you had.

MARTIN. I can't stop the mouth of the whole world.

TETZEL. Why, your heresy isn't even original. It's no different from Wyclif or Hus.

CAJETAN. True enough, but we mustn't try to deprive the learned doctor of his originality. It is original so long as it originated in *you,* the virgin heretic.

TETZEL. The time'll come when you'll have to defend yourself before the world, and then every man can judge for himself who's the heretic and schismatic. People like you always go too far, thank Heaven. I give you a month, Brother Martin, to roast yourself.

MARTIN. You've had your thirty pieces of silver. For the sake of Christ, why don't you go and betray someone?

TETZEL. How dare you!

CAJETAN [*to* TETZEL]. Tetzel, perhaps you should join Staupitz.

TETZEL. Very well, your eminence. [*He bows and goes out* D L.]

CAJETAN [*looking after* TETZEL]. In point of fact, he gets eighty guilden a month plus expenses.

MARTIN. What about his vow of poverty?

CAJETAN. Like most brilliant men, my son, you have an innocent spirit. I've also learned that he has managed to father two children. So there goes another vow. Bang! But it'll do him no good, I promise you. You've made a hole in that drum for him. I may say there's a lot of bad feelings among the Dominicans about you. I should know—because I'm their General. It's only natural; they're accustomed to having everything their own way. The Franciscans are a grubby, sentimental lot, on the whole, and mercifully ignorant as well. [*Crossing to chair.*] But your people seem to be running alive with scholars and would-be politicians.

MARTIN. I'd no idea that my theses would ever get such publicity.

CAJETAN [*sitting*]. Really, now!

MARTIN. But it seems they've been printed over and over again, and circulated well, to an extent I'd never dreamed of.

CAJETAN. Oh, yes, they've been circulated and talked about wherever men kneel to Christ.

MARTIN [*stepping to* CAJETAN, *kneeling on both knees*]. Most holy father, I honor the Holy Roman Church, and I shall go on doing so. I have sought after the truth, and everything I have said I still believe to be right and true and Christian. But I am a man, and I may be deceived, so I am willing to receive instruction where I have been mistaken.

CAJETAN [*angrily*]. Save your arrogance, my son, there'll be a better place to use it. I can have you sent to Rome, and let any of your German princes try to stop me! He'll find himself standing outside the gates of Heaven like a leper.

MARTIN [*stung, rising*]. I repeat, I am here to reply to all the charges you may bring against me——

CAJETAN. No, you're not——

MARTIN. I am ready to submit my theses to the universities of Basle, Freibourg-im-Breisgau, Louvain or Paris——

CAJETAN. I'm afraid you've not understood the position. I'm not here to enter into a disputation with you, now or at any other time. The Roman Church is the apex of the world, spiritual and temporal, and it may constrain with its secular arm any of those who have once received the faith and gone astray. Surely, I don't have to remind you that it is not bound to use reason to fight and destroy rebels. [*Suddenly aware of his angry outburst, collects himself and continues calmly.*] My son, it's getting late. You must retract. Believe me, I simply want to see this business ended as quickly as possible.

MARTIN. Some interests are furthered by finding truth, others by destroying it. I don't care—what pleases or displeases the Pope. He is a man.

CAJETAN [*wearily*]. Is that all?

MARTIN. He seems a good man, as popes go. But it's not much for a world that sings out for reformation.

CAJETAN. All right, Martin, I *will* argue with you if you want me to—or rather, I'll put something to you, because there is something more than your safety or your life involved, something bigger than you and me talking together in this room at this time. Oh, it's fine for someone like you to criticize and start tearing down Christendom, but tell me this, what will you build in its place?

MARTIN. An infected place is best scoured out, and so you pray for healthy tissue and something sturdy and clean for what was crumbling and full of filth.

CAJETAN. My dear son, don't you see? You would destroy the perfect unity of the world.

MARTIN. Someone always prefers what's withered and infected. But it should be cauterized as honestly as one knows how.

CAJETAN. And how honest is that? [*Rising, crosses* R, *around and above chair.*] There's something I'd like to know. Suppose you did destroy the Pope. What do you think would become of you?

MARTIN. I don't know.

CAJETAN. Exactly, you wouldn't know what to do because you need him, Martin, you need to hunt him more than he needs his silly wild boar. Well? There have always been popes, and there always will be even if they're called something else. They'll have them for people like *you*. You're not a good old revolutionary, my son, you're just a common rebel, a very different animal. You fight the Pope, not because he's too big, but because for your needs he's not big enough.

MARTIN. My General's been gossiping——

CAJETAN [*contemptuous*]. I don't need Staupitz to explain you to me. Why, some poor, deluded creature might even come to you as a leader of their revolution, but you don't want to break rules, you want to make them. I've read some of your sermons on faith. Do you know all they say to me?

MARTIN. No.

CAJETAN [*crossing to* MARTIN]. They say: I am a man struggling for certainty, struggling insanely like a man in a fit, an animal trapped to the bone with doubt.

MARTIN [*turning away, crossing* D L]. Your eminence, forgive me. I'm tired after my journey—I think I might faint soon——

CAJETAN [*following*]. Don't you see what could happen out of all of this? Men could be cast out and left to themselves forever, helpless and frightened! That's what would become of them without their Mother Church—with all its imperfections, Peter's rock. Without it they'd be helpless and unprotected. Allow them their sins, my son, their petty indulgences, they're unimportant to the comfort we receive——

MARTIN [*somewhat hysterical, turning to* CAJETAN]. Comfort! It—doesn't concern me!

CAJETAN. We live in thick darkness, and it grows thicker. How will men find God if they are left to themselves, each man abandoned and only known to himself?

MARTIN. They'll have to try.

CAJETAN. I beg of you, my son, I beg of you. Retract. [*Pause.*]

MARTIN. Most worthy father, I cannot. [*Pause.*]

CAJETAN. You look ill. You had better go and rest. [*Pause. Crossing* R *to chair.*] Naturally, you will be released from your order.

MARTIN. I——

CAJETAN [*turning back*]. Yes?

MARTIN. As you say, your eminence. Will you refer this matter to the Pope for his decision?

CAJETAN [*arc to* C, *facing front*]. Assuredly. Send in Tetzel. [MARTIN *crosses to* CAJETAN, *kisses ring, then bows to floor. As he kneels up,* CAJETAN *places his hand on Martin's head.*] You know, Martin, a time will come when a man will no longer be able to say "I speak Latin and am a Christian" and go his way in peace. There will come frontiers, barriers of all kinds—between men—and there'll be no end of them.

[MARTIN *rises with difficulty.* CAJETAN *assists him.* MARTIN *backs out.* TETZEL *returns.*]

TETZEL. Yes?

CAJETAN. No, of course he didn't—that man hates himself. And if he goes to the stake, Tetzel, you can have the pleasure of inscribing it: He could only love others. [*Turns and exits* R *as lights fade.*]

ACT TWO

Scene Five

SCENE: *Hunting horns are heard as though from different parts of a forest. Lights build to reveal a large, ornately framed panel stage* R *which contains a tapestry-like hunting scene. At the top of the panel are suspended the arms, the brass balls, of the Medici. In front of the panel is a carved folding chair with tooled leather seat and back. The* KNIGHT *sweeps downstage and circles* L, *banner flying.*

KNIGHT. A Hunting Lodge, Magliana, Northern Italy.

[*Amid offstage cries and shouts, the Pope's retinue enters briskly from* D L, *led by two attendants with prancing wolf-hounds, one moving* U R, *the other taking position left of the chair. Another huntsman carrying a carved T-shaped perch with two hooded falcons crosses to* D R, *and a fourth carrying a crossbow, quiver with arrows, and the Pope's black leather gauntlets takes position at the right of the chair.* MILTITZ *enters from* U R *and takes position right of the* KNIGHT, *who surveys the scene from* C.]

KNIGHT. Karl von Miltitz, Chamberlain of the Pope's household. [*The* KNIGHT *steps smartly downstage and faces* L.] Pope Leo the Tenth.

[*The* KNIGHT *exits* U L *as the* POPE *sweeps in, richly dressed in hunting clothes, long boots, plumed hat, and cape. He is followed by his secretary, a Dominican, who carries a writing board which contains ink and quill and a jeweled reading glass. The Pope is indolent, cultured, intelligent, extremely restless, and well able to assimilate the essence of anything before anyone else. While he is listening, he is able*

to play with the birds or dogs, or take practice aims with the
crossbow. As he reaches center stage, MILTITZ *meets him,*
kneeling to kiss the Pope's ring, and then bends to the toe.
The horns fade.]

LEO. I should forget it. I've got my boots on. [*Crossing to*
chair and sitting.] Well! Get on with it. We're missing the
good weather. [MILTITZ *has a letter in his belt, which he*
reads.]

MILTITZ. "To the most blessed father Leo the Tenth, sovereign
bishop, Martin Luther, Augustine friar, wishes eternal salvation. I am told that there are vicious reports circulating
about me, and that my name is in bad odor with your holiness. I am called a heretic, apostate, traitor and many other
insulting names. I cannot understand all this hostility, and
I am alarmed by it. But the only basis of my tranquility remains, as always, a pure and peaceful conscience. [LEO *snorts*
abstractedly.] Deign to listen to me, most holy father, to
me who is like a child.

[LEO *rises impatiently, snaps fingers for crossbow which he*
cocks, then extends hand for arrow which he fixes in place,
and stands scanning horizon D L.]

"There have always been, as long as I can remember, com-
plaints and grumbling in the taverns about the avarice of
the priests and attacks on the power of the keys. And this
has been happening throughout Germany. When I listened
to these things my zeal was aroused for the glory of Christ,
so I warned not one, but several princes of the Church.
[LEO *starts across* R.] But, either they laughed in my face
or ignored me. The terror of your name was too much for
everyone. [LEO *stops at this, then proceeds* U R, *scanning*
for game and taking aim.] It was then I published my disputation, nailing it on the door of the Castle Church here
in Wittenberg. And now, most holy father, the whole world
has gone up in flames. Tell me what I should do? I cannot
retract—[LEO *whips around.* MILTITZ, *occupied with the let-*
ter, reads on.]—but this thing has drawn down hatred on me

from all sides, and I don't know where to turn to but to you.
I am far too insignificant to appear before the world in a
matter as great as this.

[LEO *snaps his fingers to glance at this passage in the letter.
The secretary crosses to* LEO, *hands him a jeweled reading
glass, and clears* U C. LEO *reads, and returns letter to* MIL-
TITZ, *who continues reading.* LEO *moves* D C.]

"But in order to quiet my enemies and satisfy my friends,
I am now addressing myself to you, most holy father, and
speak my mind in the greater safety of the shadow of your
wings. [LEO *crosses to bird* D R *and strokes feathers.*] All
this respect I show to the power of the keys. If I had not
behaved properly, it would have been impossible for the
most serene Lord Frederick, Duke and Elector of Saxony,
who shines in your apostolic favor, to have endured me in
his University of Wittenberg. Not if I am as dangerous as
is made out by my enemies. [LEO *crosses back to dog* U R
and stands patting till end of letter.] For this reason, most
holy father, I fall at the feet of your holiness, and submit
myself to you, with all I have and all that I am. Declare me
right or wrong. Take my life, or give it back to me, as you
please. Written the day of the Holy Trinity in the year 1518,
Martin Luther, Augustine Friar."

[*They wait for* LEO *to finish his playing and give them his
full attention. He crosses* D C *thoughtfully, concealing his
feelings until he speaks.*]

LEO. Double-faced German bastard! Why can't he say what he
means? [*Handing glass back to secretary.*] What else?
[*Crossing to sit.*]

MILTITZ. He's said he's willing to be judged by any of the
universities of Germany, except Leipzig, Erfurt and Frank-
furt, which he says are not impartial. He says it's impossible
for him to appear in Rome in person.

LEO. I'm sure.

MILTITZ. Because his health wouldn't stand up to the rigors of
the journey.

LEO. Cunning! Cunning German bastard! What does Staupitz say for him?

MILTITZ. "The reverend father, Martin Luther, is the noblest and most distinguished member of our university. For years, we have watched his talents——"

LEO. Yes, well, we know all about that. Write to Cajetan. Take this down. We charge you to summon before you once more, Martin Luther. This time, invoke for this purpose, the aid of our very dear son in Christ, Maximilian, and all the other princes in Germany, together with all communities, universities, potentates ecclesiastic and secular. Once you get possession of him, keep him in safe custody, so that he may be brought before us. [*Rises, snaps for gauntlets, which he puts on.*] If, however, he should return to his duty of his own accord and begs forgiveness, we give you the power to receive him into the perfect unity of our Holy Mother the Church. [*Crossing* R.] But, should he persist in his obstinacy and you cannot secure him, we authorize you to outlaw him in every part of Germany. To banish and excommunicate him. [MILTITZ, *appalled, starts to interject, but* LEO *whirls on him with pointed emphasis.*] Together with all persons of rank who do not assist in apprehending him. [LEO *continues cross* R *to bird. Taking tether ring in left hand and bird on right wrist.*] As for the laymen, if they do not immediately obey your orders, declare them infamous, deprived of Christian burial and stripped of anything they may hold either from the apostolic see or from any lord whatsoever. There's a wild pig in our vineyard, and it must be hunted down and shot. Given under the seal of the Fisherman's Ring, et cetera. That is all! [*Makes a sweeping exit* U R. *The hunting horns flare up as lights fade to blackout.*]

ACT TWO

Scene Six

SCENE: *The ominous tolling of a great bell mingles with the fading hunting horns. The bell continues as lights come up on a large replica of the decorative cover page of the Papal Bull suspended* U C. *The pulpit is now* D R *with the steps swiveled to face the audience.* MARTIN *hurtles on stage, bull in hand, ascending the pulpit as the bell fades.*]

MARTIN. I have been served with a piece of paper. Let me tell you about it. It has come from a latrine called Rome. It is called the papal bull and it claims to excommunicate me, Dr. Martin Luther. These lies they rise up from this screed like fumes from the bog of Europe; because papal decretals are the devil's excretals. I'll hold it up for you to see properly. You see the signature? Signed beneath the seal of the Fisherman's Ring by one certain midden cock called Leo, an overindulged jakes' attendant to Satan himself, a glittering worm in excrement, known to you as his holiness the Pope. You may know him as the head of the Church. Which he may still be: Like a fish is the head of a cat's dinner, eyes without sight clutched to a stick of sucked bones. God has told me: there can be no dealings between this cat's dinner and me. And, as for this bull, it's going to roast, it's going to roast and so are the balls of the Medici! [MARTIN *thrusts the bull overhead and rips it in half. There is thunder and an outburst of dissonant chords from an offstage choir.* MARTIN *gasps, whirls in the pulpit as though struck, and half falls, half stumbles from the pulpit, swinging from the rail as he drops to the floor and crouches at the side of the steps. The lights on the bull and pulpit fade as lights from* D L *and* D R *illuminate the kneeling* MARTIN, *casting great shad-*

ows on the side walls.] Oh, God! Oh, God! Oh, thou my God, my God, help me against the reason and wisdom of the world. You must—there's only you—to do it. This cause is not mine but yours. For myself, I've no business to be dealing with the great lords of this world. I want to be still, in peace, and alone. My God, my God, do you hear me? Are you dead? Are you dead? No, you can't die, you can only hide yourself, can't you? Lord, I'm afraid. Breathe into me, in the name of Thy Son, Jesus Christ, who shall be my protector and defender, yes, my mighty fortress. Give me life, O Lord. Give me life.

CURTAIN

ACT THREE

Scene One

AT RISE OF CURTAIN: *The* KNIGHT *is discovered in his shaft of light* D L.]

KNIGHT. The Diet of Worms, fifteen hundred and twenty-one.

[*Accompanied by an orchestral fanfare played on antique instruments, the lights build on a gold scrim in an ornate frame. On it, in the brightest sunshine of color, a bold, joyous representation of a unique gathering of princes, electors, dukes, ambassadors, bishops, counts, barons, etc.—the medieval world dressed up for the Renaissance. The* KNIGHT *crosses to* C, *where there is a table laden with the clumsy books of the period. There are tall carved chairs, each with a small table at its side,* D L *and* D R. ECK *enters from* D R *and stands looking thoughtfully at the right chair as light continues to build.*]

KNIGHT. Johan von Eck, Chancellor of Ingolstadt.

[*The* KNIGHT *exits* U R. *The processional music continues.* ECK *crosses to the left chair where he is met by nobles and scholars. The* ARCHBISHOP *of Trier enters from* R *and joins the group. The nobles and* ECK *bow, and conversation continues. One noble notices* MARTIN *entering from* L, *and all turn to watch as he proceeds stolidly across to the chair* R *followed by* STAUPITZ *and* WEINAND, *both anxious and apprehensive. The three black figures stand out in sharp and lonely contrast to the richly robed nobles and churchmen. A* HERALD *enters from* L, *crosses to* C, *and facing the audience, thumps a mace three times. The group on stage face front.*]

HERALD. His Imperial Majesty, Charles the Fifth.

[*All bow deeply to the Emperor who would seem to be placed*

in the theatre balcony center. The music swells to a conclu-
sion as MARTIN *sits* R *with* WEINAND *and* STAUPITZ *at his*
right. The nobles and churchmen are arranged back of ECK
on the left. Music ends. ECK *rises.*]

ECK [*rising*]. Martin Luther, you were brought here by His
Imperial Majesty so that you may answer two questions.
When I asked you yesterday if you'd publicly acknowledge
being the author of the books, you agreed immediately that
the books were indeed your own. Is that right? [MARTIN
nods in agreement.] When I asked you the second question,
you asked if you might be allowed time in which to consider
it. Although such time should have been quite unnecessary
for an experienced debater and distinguished doctor of theology like yourself, His Imperial Majesty was graciously
pleased to grant your request. Well, you have had your time
now, a whole day and a night, and so I will repeat the question to you. [*Back to books.*] Do you mean to defend all
these books, or will you retract any of them? [ECK *sits.* MAR-
TIN *rises and speaks with great deliberation, passionately
making point after point—a man arguing for his life.*]

MARTIN. Your serene Majesty, most illustrious princes and
gracious lords, I appear before you by God's mercy, and I
beg that you will listen patiently. If, through my ignorance,
I have not given anyone his proper title or offended in any
way against the etiquette of such a place as this, I ask your
pardon in advance for a man who finds it hard to know his
way outside the few steps from wall to wall of a monk's
cell. [*Moves* U C *to table.*] I ask your serene Majesty and
your gracious lordships to take note that not all my books
are of the same kind. For instance, in the first group, I have
dealt quite simply with the values of faith and morality, and
even my enemies have agreed that all this is quite harmless,
and can be read without damaging the most fragile Christian. If I'm to begin by withdrawing these books, what
should I be doing? I should be condemning those very
things my friends and enemies are agreed on. [*Moving*
D C.] There is a second group of books I have written, and

these all attack the power of the keys, which has ravaged Christendom. No one can deny this, the evidence is everywhere and everyone complains of it. And no one has suffered more from this tyranny than the Germans. They have been plundered without mercy. If I were to retract those books now, I should be issuing a license for more tyranny, and it is too much to ask of me.

[*Struggling to regain a calm approach, he moves back to table.*]

I have also written a third kind of book against certain private, distinguished, and, apparently—high established—individuals. In these books, it's possible that I have been more violent than may seem necessary, or, shall I say, tasteful in one who is, after all, a monk. But then, I have never set out to be a saint, and I've not been defending my own life, but the teaching of Christ. So again I'm not free to retract. [*Moving* D C *as though speaking directly to Emperor.*] What I ask, by the Mercy of God, is let someone expose my errors in the light of the Gospels. The moment you have done this, I shall ask you to let me be the first to pick up my books and hurl them in the fire. That is all. [*Crosses to chair and sits.*]

ECK [*rising*]. Martin, you have not answered the question put to you. Even if it were true that some of your books are innocuous—a point which, incidentally, we don't concede— we still ask that you cut out these passages which are— [*Crossing to table.*]—blasphemous; that you cut out the heresies or whatever could be construed as heresy, and, in fact, that you delete any passage which might be considered hurtful to the Catholic faith. His sacred and imperial Majesty—[*To* C.]—is more than prepared to be lenient. If, however—[*Crosses* R *to* MARTIN.]—you persist in your attitude, there can be no question that all memory of you will be blotted out, and everything you have written, right or wrong, will be forgotten. You see, Martin, like all heretics, you demand to be contradicted from Scripture. [*Crossing* L.]

We can only believe that you must be ill or mad. Do reasons have to be given to anyone who cares to ask a question? Why, if anyone who questioned the common understanding of the Church on any matter he liked to raise, had to be answered irrefutably from the Scriptures, there would be nothing certain or decided in Christendom. What would the Jews and Turks and Saracens say if they heard us *debating* whether what we have always believed is true or not? I beg you, Martin, not to believe that you—[*Crossing to* MAR-TIN.]—and you alone, understand the meaning of the Gospels. Don't throw doubt on the most holy, orthodox faith, the faith founded by the most perfect legislator known to us. It is our heritage, and we are forbidden to dispute it by the laws of the emperor and the pontiff. [*Crossing* L.] I must, therefore, ask again, I must demand that you answer sincerely, frankly and unambiguously, yes or no—[*Turning to* MARTIN.]—will you or will you not retract your books and the errors contained in them. [*Sits.*]

MARTIN [*rising—pale, tense but controlled, crossing to table*]. Since your serene Majesty and your lordships demand a simple answer, you shall have it, without horns and without teeth. Unless I am shown by the testimony of the Scriptures—[*With rising fervor.*]—for I don't believe in popes or councils—unless I am refuted by Scripture and my conscience is captured by God's own word, I cannot and will not recant, since to act against one's conscience—[*Picks up book from table.*]—is neither safe nor honest. [*Thrusts book overhead.*] Here I stand; God help me; I can do no more. Amen.

[*There is a roll of drums, the lights fade, leaving* MARTIN *in a single spot. The chairs and small tables disappear with the monks and nobles. The drum roll subsides into a definite beat and there is a hushed and guttural sound of the "Eine Feste Burg," half sung, half talked, in German. Lights behind the scrim gradually reveal a row of* PEASANTS *in rags. They are hunched and bent, as though tilling the soil. As*

*the song continues they slowly straighten. What seemed to
be hoes and rakes become banners, tattered and bearing the
Bundschuh emblem. They are held like spears. The scrim
slowly rises and the* PEASANTS *creep forward in the shadows. Others join from the upstage entrances, filling the stage
to form a line on a level with* MARTIN, *who is still etched
in the single light. At the end of the German verse, the
stage blacks out,* MARTIN *disappears. The* PEASANTS *stride
forward to the foots and into light from directly overhead,
banners held high. They sing loudly in English, with surg-
ing lusty determination symbolizing the peak of the peasants' revolt. The song diminishes, and the line breaks up,
falling back and to* L. *The banners sag, some drag along the
ground. The* PEASANTS *limp away in an atmosphere of utter
defeat, exhaustion, and hopelessness. The light fades downstage and slowly builds* L, *where there is a two-wheeled cart
laden with the bloody corpse of a young boy. Three battered
and wounded peasants huddle against the cart. The pulpit is*
D R; *the table and books from the previous scene have been
removed. The* KNIGHT *stands* C, *staring down at the peasants. He is without banner, helmet, or gauntlets. He is
stained and dirty.*]

ACT THREE

Scene Two

SCENE: *The* KNIGHT *suddenly turns on the audience, as the
last strains of the "Eine Feste Burg" fade away, in a defen-
sive, angry outburst. It is the passionate cry of a man once
inspired beyond his dreams and then betrayed by the very
source of his inspiration.*]

KNIGHT. There was excitement that day. In Worms—that day four long years ago. A lot's happened since then. There's no excitement like that any more. Not unless murder's your idea of excitement. I tell you, you can't have ever known the kind of thrill that monk set off amongst that collection of all kinds of men gathered together there. We all felt it, every one of us, just without any exception. You couldn't help it, even if you didn't want to, and, believe me, most of those people didn't want to. His scalp looked blotchy and itchy, and you felt sure, just looking at him, his body must be permanently sour and white all over, even whiter than his face and like a millstone to touch. He'd sweated so much by the time he'd finished, I could smell every inch of him from where I was. But he fizzed like a hot spark in a trail of gunpowder going off in us, that dowdy monk, he went off in us, and nothing could stop it, and it blew up and there was nothing we could do, any of us, that was it. Neither the Emperor nor the Pope dared to lay a hand on him. I just felt quite sure, quite certain in my own mind, nothing could ever be the same again. Something had taken place, an event had occurred in the flesh, in the flesh and the breath—like, even like when the weight of that body slumped on its wooden crotch-piece and the earth grew dark. That's the kind of thing I mean by happen. I don't think even if I could speak and write like him, I could begin to give you an idea of what we thought, of what we might come to. Obviously, we couldn't have all felt quite the same way, but I wanted to burst my ears with shouting and draw my sword, no, not draw it, I wanted to pluck it as if it were a flower in my blood and plunge it into whatever he would have told me to.

[*One of the peasants plays a few mournful notes of "Eine Feste Burg" on a wooden flute.*]

And I wasn't the only one. The peasants of Swabia rose up and demanded an end to their serfdom. He encouraged them till they took up arms, then he wrote an appeal for their ex-

termination. If only one could understand him. I just can't
make him out.

[*Turning to corpse.*]

Anyway, it never worked out. Did it, my friend? Not the
way we expected, anyway, certainly not the way *you* expected—but who'd have ever thought we might end up
on different sides, Luther on one and us on the other. That
when the war came between you and them, he'd be there
beating the drum for *them* outside the slaughter house, and
beating it louder and better than anyone else, hollering for
your blood, cutting you up in your thousands, and hanging
you up to drip away into the fire for good.

[*The* PEASANTS *drag themselves up and slowly exit* U R.
The KNIGHT *crosses* D L.]

They were all the same, all those big princes and archbish-
ops, the cut-rate nobility and rich layabouts, honorable this
and thats scrabbling like boars 'round a swill bucket for
every penny those poor peasants never had. All those great
abbots with their dewlaps dropped and hanging on their
necks like goose's eggs, and those leftover knights, like me
for instance, I suppose, who'd seen better days and were
scared and'd stop at nothing to try to make sure they
couldn't get any worse. Yes. . . . Not one of them could
read the words "THIS WAY OUT" when it was written up
for them, marked out clearly and unmistakably in the pain
of too many men. Yes. [*Crosses to* C.] They say, you know,
that the profit motive—and I'm sure you know all about
that one—they say the profit motive was born with the in-
vention of double entry bookkeeping in the monasteries,
ages before any of us had ever got 'round to burning them
down. But, you know, for men with such a motive, there
is really only one entry. The profit is theirs, the loss is someone else's, and usually they don't even bother to write it up.

[*Crosses up to corpse.*]

Well, it was your old loss, wasn't it, my friend, your dead
loss, in fact. You could say his life was more or less a write-

off right from the day he was born. He—and all the others
like him, everywhere, now and after him.

[MARTIN *enters* U L, *wearing a white alb over a black knee-
length robe, black shoes and leggings. His hair, slightly
greyed, has grown out, the tonsure gone. He is older, heav-
ier. He genuflects* D L *as he did at the opening of Act Two,
Scene Three. He carries a Bible. The* KNIGHT *watches, then
picks up the cart and wheels it roughly to Martin's feet as
he rises.*]

KNIGHT. There! You even look like a butcher——

MARTIN. God is the butcher—— Why don't you address your
abuse to Him?

KNIGHT. Never mind—you're wearing His apron. [*Pause.*]
All you've ever managed to do is convert everything into
stench and dying and peril, but you could have done it, you
alone could have done it. Martin, you could have brought
freedom and order in at one and the same time.

MARTIN. There's no such thing as an orderly revolution.
[*Crossing below cart, past* KNIGHT *to* C.] Anyway, Christians are called upon to suffer, not fight.

KNIGHT. But weren't we all of us, all of us, redeemed by
Christ's blood? Wasn't he included when the Scriptures
were being dictated? Or was it just you who was made free,
you and the princes you've taken up with?

MARTIN [*whirling on* KNIGHT]. Free? The princes blame me,
you blame me, and the peasants blame me——

KNIGHT. *You* put the water in the wine, didn't you?

MARTIN. When I see chaos I see the devil's organ and then
I'm afraid. Now, that's enough—— [*Turning toward pulpit.*]

KNIGHT [*following*]. You're breaking out again——

MARTIN [*ascending pulpit steps*]. Go away.

KNIGHT. Aren't you?

MARTIN. Get back!

KNIGHT. Aren't you, you're breaking out again, you canting
pig, I can smell you from here!

MARTIN [*stopping halfway up steps*]. He heard the children of Israel, didn't He?

KNIGHT. Up to the ears in revelation, aren't you?

MARTIN And didn't He deliver them out of the Land of Pharaoh?

KNIGHT. You're a canting pig, aren't you?

MARTIN. Well? Didn't He?

KNIGHT. Cock's wounds! Don't hold your Bible to my head, piggy. There's enough revelation of my own in there for me —in what I see for myself from here. [*Taps his forehead.*] Weigh your Gospel against that. [*The* KNIGHT *grabs* MARTIN's *hand and clamps it to his head.*] There! Now you've got your hand against it, that's all the holy spirit there is, and it's all you'll ever get, so feel it. [*They struggle, and* MARTIN *is able to wrench himself away and up into the pulpit.*]

MARTIN. The world has conquered by the Word, the Church is maintained by the Word——

KNIGHT. Word? What Word? Do you know what most men believe, Martin? In their hearts they believe that Christ was a man as they are, and that he was a prophet and a teacher, that his supper was a plain meal like their own—if they're lucky enough to get it—a plain meal of bread and wine! . . . with no garnish and no Word. And *you* helped them to begin to believe it!

MARTIN [*pause*]. Leave me.

KNIGHT [*crossing to cart, starting to wheel it off* U R]. Yes. What's there to stay for? I've been close enough to you for too long. I even smell like you.

MARTIN [*roaring with pain, stopping* KNIGHT *at* C]. I smell because of my own argument. I smell because I never stop disputing with Him, and because I expect Him to keep his Word. Now then! If your peasant rebelled against that Word, that was worse than murder because it laid the whole country waste, and who knows now what God will make of us Germans!

KNIGHT. Don't blame God for the Germans, Martin!

[*Laughs.*] You thrashed about more than anyone on the
night they were conceived!

MARTIN. Christ! Hear me! My words pour from Your Body!
They deserved their death, these swarming peasants! They
kicked against authority, they plundered and bargained and
all in Your name! Christ, believe me! [*To* KNIGHT.] They
were a mob—a mob! And if they had not been held down
and slaughtered, there would have been a thousand more
tyrants, instead of half a dozen! I prayed for it. I demanded
it. And I got it! [*The* KNIGHT, *defeated, turns and wearily
moves* L *to collect tattered banner* (*breakaway*) *left by one
of the peasants.* MARTIN *watches as he returns to lay it on
cart, then begins one more anxious attempt for understanding.*] I expect you must . . . I'm sure you must remember
—Abraham . . . Abraham was an old man . . . a very
old man—[*Out of pulpit.*]—indeed, in fact, he was a hundred years old, when what surely must have been a miracle
happened, to a man of his years—a son was born to him. A
son. Isaac, he called him. And he loved Isaac. Well, he loved
him with such intensity, one can only diminish it by de-
scription. But to Abraham his little son was a miraculous
thing, a small, incessant . . . animal astonishment. And in
the child he sought the father. But, one day, God said to
Abraham: Take your little son whom you love so much,
kill him, and make a sacrifice of him. And in that moment
everything inside Abraham seemed to shrivel once and for
.all. Because it had seemed to him that God had promised
him life through his son. [*Crosses to stand at cart.*] But he
took the boy and prepared to kill him, strapping him down
to the wood of the burnt offering just as he had been told
to do. And he spoke softly to the boy, and raised the knife
over his little naked body, the boy struggling not to flinch
or blink his eyes. Never, save in Christ, was there such
obedience as in that moment, and if God had blinked, the
boy would have died then, but the Angel intervened, and
the boy was released, and Abraham took him up in his arms
again. [*Crosses to* KNIGHT.] In the teeth of life we seem to

die, but God say
butchers us, He
Drag it away witl

[*The* KNIGHT *cros*
the cart, but stop
Martin's future u
ing girl, almost
She stops when s
tin's weary figure
stand on the revo
MARTIN *and hel*
cloak. The KNIGH

84

tive darkness. Martin's
pain of middle age
anticipated happ
pitz a worried
with both
but the
two

KNIGHT. All right, my friend. Stay with your nun, then. Marry
and stew with your nun, like a shuddering infant in *her* bed.
You think you'll manage?
MARTIN [*with irony*]. At least my father'll praise me for *that*.
[*Exits with* KATHERINE *at his left*.]
KNIGHT. Your father?

[*Light fades, leaving* KNIGHT *in single lonely light. He stares
at the tattered banner, then with a cry of frustration smashes
it across his knee.*]

ACT THREE

Scene Three

SCENE: *There is the sound of a simple melody being played
on a lute. The lights come up on the stage* L *area, revealing
a tall desk where* MARTIN *stands brooding over papers.
There are two wooden armchairs at either side, but downstage of the desk. The pulpit remains at stage* R, *but in rela-*

*earlier vigor has settled into the tired
, struggling to rediscover strength. An
reunion has gone awry in finding Stau-
and saddened old man. MARTIN tries gamely,
atherine and Staupitz, to brighten the occasion,
vents of recent years lie heavily between them. The
en must finally face their truths. KATHERINE enters
two wooden mugs which she places on desk.]*

KATHERINE. I've brought you some more wine. It'll help you
to sleep.

MARTIN. How is Staupitz?

KATHERINE [*moving two steps down*]. He's all right. He's
just coming. Wouldn't let me help him. I think he's been
sick.

MARTIN [*joining her*]. Poor old chap. After living all your
life in a monastery, one's stomach doesn't take too easily to
your kind of cooking.

KATHERINE. You like your food, so don't make out you don't.

MARTIN. Well, I prefer it to fasting. [*Putting arm around her.*]
Did you never hear the story of the soldier who was fighting
in the Holy Crusades? No? Well, he was told by his officer
that if he died in battle, he would dine in Paradise with
Christ; and the soldier ran away. When he came back after
the battle, they asked him why he'd run away. "Didn't you
want to dine with Christ?" "No," he said. "I'm fasting today."

[STAUPITZ *enters, supporting himself with a stick.*]

MARTIN. There you are! I thought you'd fallen down the jakes
right into the devil's loving arms. [*Indicating chair* L.]
Well, come and sit down. [*As* STAUPITZ *settles down.*]
Good night, Katie. [KATHERINE *crosses* D L.]

STAUPITZ. Good night, my dear. Thank you for the dinner.
I'm sorry I wasn't able to do justice to it.

KATHERINE. That's all right. Good night, Dr. Staupitz. [*She
curtsies and goes out.*]

STAUPITZ. Well, *you've* never been so well looked after.

MARTIN. It's a shame everyone can't marry a nun. They're fine cooks, thrifty housekeepers and splendid mothers. Seems to me there are three ways out to despair. One is faith in Christ, the second is to become enraged by the world and make its nose bleed for it, and the third is the love of a woman. Mind you, they don't all necessarily work—at least, only part of the time. [*Crosses to desk.*] Wine?

STAUPITZ. Not much. I must go to bed myself.

MARTIN [*giving mug to* STAUPITZ]. It'll help you sleep. You're looking tired.

STAUPITZ. Old. Martin, I can't get over being here again. This place was full of men, and now there's only you—you and Katie. It's so still. I don't think I'd ever realized how eloquent a monk's silence really was. It was a voice. . . . It's gone.

MARTIN. My old friend, you're unhappy. I'm sorry. [*Pause. Crosses to* C.] We monks were never any good to anyone, least of all to ourselves, every one of us rolled up like a louse in the Almighty's overcoat.

STAUPITZ. You always had a way of putting it.

MARTIN [*turning back*]. Father, are you pleased with me?

STAUPITZ. I? Pleased with you? My dear son, I'm not anyone or anything to be pleased with you any more. Every time you belch now, the world stops what it's doing and listens. I'm sorry, Martin. I didn't mean to come and see you after all this time and start criticizing.

MARTIN. Don't upset yourself. I'm used to critics. They help you to keep your muscles from getting slack. [*Pause. Crossing to* R *of right chair.*] But why are you accusing me? What have I done?

STAUPITZ. I'm not accusing you, Martin. You know that. A just man is his own accuser. Because a just man judges himself as he is.

MARTIN. What does that mean? I'm not just?

STAUPITZ. You try. What more can you do?

MARTIN [*taking his mug to desk*]. You mean those damned

peasants, don't you? You think I should have encouraged them!

STAUPITZ. I didn't say that.

MARTIN [crossing to STAUPITZ]. Well, what do you say?

STAUPITZ. You needn't have encouraged the princes. They slaughtered those peasants and *you* got them to do it. And the peasants had just cause, Martin. They did, didn't they?

MARTIN. I didn't say they hadn't.

STAUPITZ. Well, then?

MARTIN. Do you remember saying to me, "Remember, you started this in the name of our Lord Jesus Christ"?

STAUPITZ. Well?

MARTIN [crossing C]. Father, the world can't be ruled with a rosary. It was a mob, and because it was a mob it was against Christ. [*His exasperated defense hangs in the air unanswered. Turning back, then sitting on right arm of chair, facing* R.] You're leaving me.

STAUPITZ [rising]. I'm not leaving you, Martin. I love you. I love you as much as most men have ever loved most women. But we're not two protected monks chattering under a pear tree in a garden any longer. The world's changed. [*Takes mug to desk.*] To begin with, you've made a thing called Germany; you've unlaced a language and taught it to the Germans, and the rest of the world will just have to get used to the sound of it. As we once made the body of Christ from bread, you've made the body of Europe, and whatever your pains turn out to be, they'll attack the rest of the world, too. You've taken Christ away from the low mumblings and soft voices and jeweled gowns and the tiaras and put Him back where He belongs. In each man's soul. We owe so much to you. All I beg of you is not to be too violent. In spite of everything, of everything you've said and shown us, there *were* men, *some* men who did live holy lives here once. Don't—don't believe that you, only you are right. [STAUPITZ *is close to tears.*]

MARTIN. What can I do, John? What can I do?

STAUPITZ. When you were before the Diet in Worms, and

they put that question to you—why did you ask for that extra day to think over your reply? [*Pause.*]

MARTIN. I wasn't certain.

STAUPITZ. And were you? Afterwards?

MARTIN. I listened for God's voice, but all I could hear was my own.

STAUPITZ. *Were* you sure?

MARTIN [*turning head slowly to* STAUPITZ]. No.

STAUPITZ [*crossing, laying hand on Martin's shoulder*]. Thank you, my son. May God bless you. [*Turns, exiting* D L.] I hope you sleep better. Good night.

MARTIN. Good night, Father. [STAUPITZ *goes out, and* MARTIN *is left alone. The mournful cello from Act One is heard.*] Oh, Lord, I believe. I believe. I do believe. Only help my unbelief.

[*The music fades as* KATHERINE *enters. She is wearing a night-dress, and carries in her arms, Hans, their young son.*]

KATHERINE. He was crying out in his sleep. Must have been dreaming again. Aren't you coming to bed?

MARTIN. Shan't be long, Katie. Shan't be long.

KATHERINE. All right, but try not to be too long. You look— well, you don't look as well as you should. [*She turns to go.*]

MARTIN. Give him to me.

KATHERINE. What? [*Turns back.*]

MARTIN. Give him to me.

KATHERINE. What do you mean, what for? He'll get cold down here.

MARTIN. No, he won't. Please, Katie. Let me have him.

KATHERINE [*giving baby to* MARTIN]. You're a funny man. All right, but only for five minutes. Don't keep him down here all night.

MARTIN. Thank you, Katie.

KATHERINE [*turning to leave*]. He's gone back to sleep now. He'll be having another dream if you keep him down here.

MARTIN. Good night, Katie.

KATHERINE. Keep him warm now! He's *your* son.

MARTIN. I will. Don't worry. [KATHERINE *goes out, leaving* MARTIN *with the sleeping child in his arms.* MARTIN *speaks softly to the child.*] What was the matter, Hans, eh? Was the devil bothering you? Um? Was he? Old Nick? Well, up you, Old Nick. Don't worry—one day you might even be glad of him. So long as you can show him your little backside. That's right, show him your backside and let him have it. [*Climbing pulpit stairs. All other lights fade.*] So try not to be afraid. The dark isn't quite as thick as all that. A little while, and you'll not see me. And again a little while, and you *shall* see me. Christ said that, my son. I hope that'll be the way of it again. I hope so. Let's just hope so, shall we? Let's just hope so.

CURTAIN

PROPERTIES

GENERAL: ACT ONE: Towering walls, gigantic crucifix. ACT TWO: Remove crucifix. Scene Two: Chair with tree branch hanging over it. Scene Three: Pulpit with stair. Scene Four: Paneled wall, painting of crucifixion, ornately carved chair, small table with two tied scrolls on it. Scene Five: Tapestry-like hunting scene in ornate frame, arms of the Medici, carved folding chair. Scene Six: Large replica of cover page of papal bull, pulpit. ACT THREE: Scene One: Gold scrim in ornate frame, a scene showing a gathering of eminent people of the time; table with groups of books of the period; two tall carved chairs, each with a small table. Scene Two: Two-wheeled cart with corpse of young boy, tattered banner. Scene Three: Desk, papers on desk, two wooden armchairs, pulpit.

KNIGHT: Helmet, gauntlets, tall staff with trailing pennant.

MONK NO. 1: Censer with burning incense; pitcher of wine.

MONK NO. 2: Brass holy water bowl and twig.

MONK NO. 4: Bible with marker, crucifix on tall staff.

MONKS NO. 5 and NO. 6: Litter containing folded mass vestments (amice, alb, stole, chasuble, maniple); large lighted candles.

WEINAND (MONK NO. 7): Martin's cassock, scapular, cowl, and belt; handkerchief in belt.

HANS: Hat, mug.

LUCAS: Hat.

MONKS: Long table set with wooden mugs and spoons, and round loaf of black bread.

A MONK: Lectern and book, leather apron, tray stacked with wooden bowls.

MARTIN: Prior's chair, leather apron, pitcher of wine (Act One); Bible, white prayer stole, papal bull (Act Two); Bible (Act Three).

MONKS NO. 2 and NO. 4: Long table with two benches on top.

MONK NO. 9: Stool.

MONK NO. 6: Mug.

MONK NO. 10: Tray with five mugs upside down on it.

MONK NO. 5: Bread, cheese and fruit on tray.

TWO CHILDREN: Finger cymbals.

DOMINICAN MONKS: Tambourines, drums, cymbals, banner with Pope's arms insignia; cart bedecked with fringes and tassels, with painting of Madonna with hovering angels, set of steps, indulgence pole, and empty chest.

TETZEL: Large red cross.

STAUPITZ: Spectacles, breviary (Act Two); cane (Act Three).

ATTENDANTS OF POPE: Wolfhounds.

HUNTSMAN: T-shaped perch with two hooded falcons.

SECOND HUNTSMAN: Crossbow and quiver of arrows, Pope's gauntlets.

SECRETARY: Writing board with ink and quill, jeweled reading glass.

MILTITZ: Letter.

HERALD: Mace.

PEASANTS: Tattered banners bearing Bundschuh emblem.

PEASANT: Wooden flute.

KATHERINE: Martin's coat, two wooden mugs, baby wrapped in blanket.

PRODUCTION NOTES

COSTUMING:

Augustinian Monks: Black cassock, scapular, cowl, leather belt with rosary hanging from it, prayer book attached to belt by a small chain, sandals. Tonsure haircut.

Dominican Monks: White habit, black cape.

Cajetan: Voluminous red cloak, helmet-like cap.

Pope: Hunting clothes, long boots, plumed hat, cape.

Martin: First appearance, coarse gray loincloth, later as an Augustinian monk, until the end of the play, when he wears a white alb over black knee-length robe, black shoes and leggings. His hair also has grown out; he no longer has tonsure cut.

Two children (Tetzel's attendants): Cassocks.

MUSIC NOTES

The following note appeared in the program of the original production of *Luther:*

"The liturgical and secular music has been chosen either from the works of Luther's contemporaries (such as Joaquin des Pres, whom Luther particularly admired) or from composers of the previous generation such as Jacob Obrecht."

. . . . .

Much of the music used in the production of *Luther* as originally produced can be found in the *Liber Usualis,* 1962 Edition, edited by the Benedictines of Solesmes; Desclee Company, Printers to the Holy See, Tournai, Belgium and New York, N. Y. When applicable, Liber page reference is given below:

1. *Veni Creator*—Liber, page 885—sung during the opening procession.
2. *Proprio Filio*—Liber, page 689—sung solo by the Cantor while garments are being blessed.
3. *Miserere Mei*—Liber, page 689—sung during the dressing of Luther.
4. *Te Deum*—Liber, page 1834—sung immediately after the Prior's prayer continuing through the "kiss of peace" ritual and off as the group exits.
5. *Deus in Adjutorium*—Liber, page 250—sung by the choir during the fit sequence.
6. *Exultet Orbis*—sung during the procession to the first mass.
7. *Kyrie*—sung offstage at the end of Act I, Scene 2—is from the Missa Fortuna Desperata by Jacob Obrecht.
8. *Ave Vera*—sung by the Tetzel retinue at the opening of Act II. Lyrics for two verses as follows:
                    Ave Vera Virginitas
                    Immaculata Castitas
                    Cujus Purificatio
                    Nostra Fuit Purgatio

Ave Praeclara Omnibus
Angelicus Virtutibus
Cujus Fuit Assumptio
Nostra Glorificatio

9. *Salve Regina*—offstage solo at the opening of Act II, Scene 2.
10. *Laudes Christo*—offstage choir at the end of Luther's sermon, Act II, Scene 3, and during the scene change.
11. *Domine—De Profundis*—offstage choir during the last half of Act II, Scene 6—was composed especially for the New York production by Max Walmer.
12. *Ein Feste Burg*—A Mighty Fortress written by Martin Luther. Sung by peasants first in German and then in English at the end of Act III, Scene 1.

SOUND EFFECTS

Organ Music—during the transition into the confession scene and at a low level during the confession, fading during Martin's last long speech.

—during the scene change leading into Act II, Scene 3.

Cello Solo—during the transition from Scene 1 to Scene 2 in Act I and continuing at a low level during the "Lost Body" soliloquy.

—on Staupitz's exit in Act III, Scene 3, and during the prayer, fading on Katherine's entrance.

Hunting Horns—during the transition into Act II, Scene 5 (Pope scene), and again at the end of the scene.

Bells—small bell or chime manually operated on cues throughout Act I.

—tolling bell cross-fades with the hunting horns leading into Act II, Scene 6.

Lute—during the transition into Act III, Scene 3.

Orchestral Fanfare—during the opening of Act III.

Bird Sounds—during Act II, Scene 2, as indicated.